THE WALKER'S LOG BOOK
Volume One

covering the Eastern, the Far Eastern
and the Central Fells

published 1955
BOOK ONE: The Eastern Fells

published 1957
BOOK TWO: The Far Eastern Fells

published 1958
BOOK THREE: The Central Fells

published 1960
BOOK FOUR: The Southern Fells

published 1962
BOOK FIVE: The Northern Fells

published 1964
BOOK SIX: The North Western Fells

published 1966
BOOK SEVEN: The Western Fells

THE WALKER'S LOG BOOK Volume Two covers the Southern, the Northern, the North Western and the Western Fells

THE WALKER'S LOG BOOK

Volume One

covering the Eastern, the Far Eastern
and the Central Fells

awainwright TM

Michael Joseph
LONDON

MICHAEL JOSEPH LTD

Published by the Penguin Group
27 Wrights Lane, London W8 5TZ
Viking Penguin Inc., 375 Hudson Street, New York,
New York 10014, USA
Penguin Books Australia Ltd, Ringwood, Victoria, Australia
Penguin Books Canada Ltd, 10 Alcorn Avenue,
Toronto, Ontario, Canada M4V 3B2
Penguin Books (NZ) Ltd, 182–190 Wairau Road,
Auckland 10, New Zealand

Penguin Books Ltd, Registered Offices: Harmondsworth,
Middlesex, England

First published in Great Britain April 1993
Second impression June 1994

Material appearing in this book is taken from works
previously published by the Westmorland Gazette, Kendal.

Typeset in Monophoto Times New Roman
Design and computer page make-up by Penny Mills
Printed in England by Clays Ltd, St Ives plc

A CIP catalogue record for this book is available
from the British Library

ISBN 0 7181 4068 0

The fleeting hour of life of those who love the hills is quickly spent, but the hills are eternal. Always there will be the lonely ridge, the dancing beck, the silent forest; always there will be the exhilaration of the summits. These are for the seeking, and those who seek and find while there is yet time will be blessed both in mind and body.

I wish you all many happy days on the fells in the years ahead.

Angletarn Pikes 1857'

from Brothers Water

From Book Two

DATE/S WALKED

ASCENT/S USED

COMMENTS (walking companions, weather, etc.)

'The crowning glory of the Pikes is the tarn from which they are named, cradled in a hollow just below the summit. Its indented shore and islets are features unusual in mountain tarns, and it has for long, and deservedly, been a special attraction.'

Armboth Fell

1570'
approx.

from Fisher Crag

Armboth Fell has probably as good a claim as any to be regarded as the most centrally situated fell in Lakeland, for straight lines drawn between the northern and southern boundaries, and between the eastern and western, would bisect hereabouts. (Since these boundaries are arbitrary, however, individual opinion will differ on this point).

Peak-baggers and record-chasers may have cause to visit the summit, but other walkers may justifiably consider its ascent a waste of precious time and energy when so many more rewarding climbs are available, for the flat desolate top is little better than a quagmire, a tangle of swamp and heather and mosses, as is much of the surrounding territory. It can be said of very few fells that they are not really worth climbing; Armboth Fell is one of the few.

HIGH SEAT
Armboth
HIGH TOVE
Watendlath
ARMBOTH FELL
Wythburn
ULLSCARF
MILES
0 1 2 3

The fell lies to the east of the central ridge, and the rain that falls upon it either elects to stay there for ever or drains slowly away towards Thirlmere, hurrying only down the steep afforested slopes immediately flanking the reservoir. Such scenic beauty as Armboth Fell has to offer is wholly concentrated in this wooded fringe above Thirlmere, where there are splendid crags and waterfalls, of which Fisher Crag and Launchy Gill are outstanding. The dark forests conceal the dying traces of a lost civilisation, lost not so very long ago.

From Book Three

DATE/S WALKED

ASCENT/S USED

COMMENTS (walking companions, weather, etc.)

'Armboth is still prominently featured on local signposts and on maps, but is now no more than a name. The Helvellyn range dominates the scene from the summit, but the best features are westwards, overtopping the central ridge.'

Arnison Crag 1424'

from Keldas

Glenridding

Patterdale

ARNISON CRAG

BIRKS

S^T SUNDAY CRAG

MILES

0 1 2

The rough fellside curving out of Deepdale and bounding the highway to Patterdale village has an attractive rocky crown, often visited for the fine view it offers of the head of Ullswater. This is Arnison Crag, a low hill with a summit worthy of a mountain. It is a dependency of St. Sunday Crag, forming the lesser of the two prongs which constitute the north-east spur of that grand fell; Birks is the other. It starts as a grass shelf east of Cold Cove and then takes the shape of a curving ridge of no particular interest except for the sudden upthrust of its craggy summit.

From Book One

DATE/S WALKED

ASCENT/S USED

COMMENTS (walking companions, weather, etc.)

'The ascent is invariably made from the village of Patterdale. Arnison Crag is surrounded by higher fells, and the view is very restricted. A feature is the fine grouping of hills above the pastures of Hartsop. Ullswater is the only lake seen.'

Arthur's Pike 1747'

from the Howtown road

From Book Two

DATE/S WALKED

ASCENT/S USED

COMMENTS (walking companions, weather, etc.)

'Arthur's Pike is the northerly termination of the long High Street range and, like the northerly termination of the Helvellyn range, it contrasts with the usual Lakeland fell-structure by exhibiting its crags to the afternoon sun.'

Beda Fell

1664'

summit named Beda Head

from Hallin Fell

Beda Fell is the long north-east ridge of Angletarn Pikes, narrowing as it descends; but midway it asserts itself, broadens considerably and rises to a definite summit, Beda Head, which is the geographical centre of the quiet, enchanting, exquisitely beautiful area known affectionately as "Martind'l."
Beyond this top the descent continues over the rocky spine of Winter Crag to valley-level at Sandwick on Ullswater.
The fell, although mainly grassy, with bracken, has a most impressive east face, broken into three great tiers of crag. It is bounded by deep valleys, Boardale, Bannerdale and Howe Grain, whose combined waters meet at its northern tip.

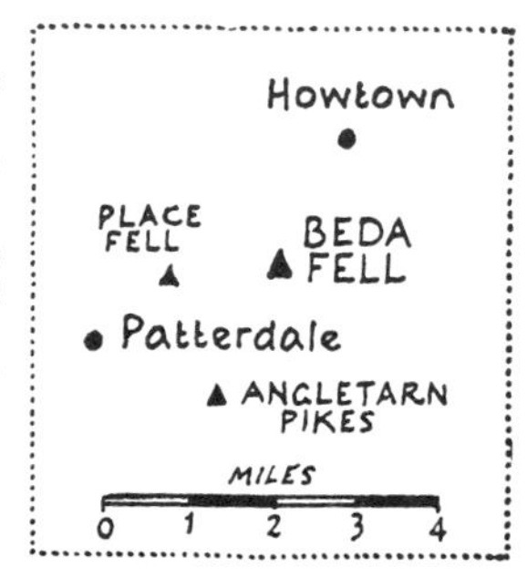

From Book Two

DATE/S WALKED

ASCENT/S USED

COMMENTS (walking companions, weather, etc.)

'Beda Fell's central position in the delectable Martindale district may have been expected to endow it with special qualities as a viewpoint, but this is not so; its upper slopes hide the beauties of the two enclosing valleys.'

Birkhouse Moor

2350'
approx.

from Lanty's Tarn

From Book One

DATE/S WALKED

ASCENT/S USED

COMMENTS (walking companions, weather, etc.)

'Birkhouse Moor falls away to the east in bracken-clad slopes, but its extremity is an abrupt wooded height overlooking Ullswater. This height is referred to as Keldas. Artists and photographers will vote Keldas the loveliest and most delightful place amongst the eastern fells.'

Birks 2040'

The north-east shoulder of St Sunday Crag falls sharply to a depression beyond which a grassy undulating spur, featureless and wide, continues with little change in elevation towards Ullswater before finally plunging down to the valley through the enclosure of Glemara Park. Although this spur lacks a distinctive summit it is sufficiently well-defined to deserve a separate name; but, being an unromantic and uninteresting fell, it has earned for itself nothing better than the prosaic and unassuming title of Birks. It is rarely visited as the sole objective of an expedition, but walkers descending the ridge from St Sunday Crag often take it in their stride.

From Book One

DATE/S WALKED ....

....

....

ASCENT/S USED ....

....

....

COMMENTS (walking companions, weather, etc.) ....

'The ascent by the Thornhow End path is very attractive, with glorious views, but it is steep. The viewpoint is a scene of strong contrasts, interesting and pleasing but not extensive.'

Bleaberry Fell 1932'

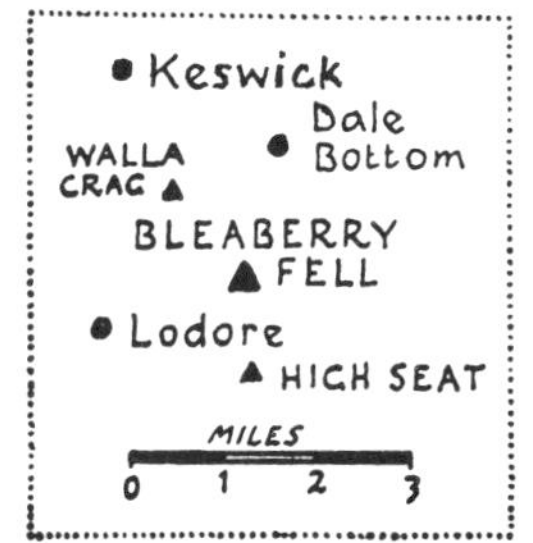

From Book Three

DATE/S WALKED ....

....

....

ASCENT/S USED ....

....

....

COMMENTS (walking companions, weather, etc.) ....

....

....

....

....

....

....

....

....

....

....

....

....

....

'Bleaberry Fell is a superb viewpoint, ideally suited for a long and lazy contemplation of a beautiful panorama. What is more, it can be climbed dryshod and the short springy heather of the top is a joy to tread.'

Blea Rigg 1776'

from Greathead Crag

From Book Three

DATE/S WALKED

ASCENT/S USED

COMMENTS (walking companions, weather, etc.)

'The Shelter Stone on the top of Blea Rigg is a useful refuge situated at the base of the prominent rocky tor 150 yards west of the summit-cairn. It cannot be seen from the path. The accommodation is strictly limited.'

Bonscale Pike 1718'

sometimes referred to as
Swarth Fell

from Hallin Fell

From Book Two

DATE/S WALKED ....

....

....

ASCENT/S USED ....

....

....

COMMENTS (walking companions, weather, etc.) ....

....

....

....

....

....

....

....

....

....

....

....

....

....

'Neither of the two stone pillars seen so prominently against the skyline from below marks the highest point, this being a grassy hummock between and behind them. The men who selected the sites of the two pillars surely had a good appreciation of drama!'

Branstree

2333'

(a corruption of Brant Street)

from the south-east ridge of High Raise

From Book Two

DATE/S WALKED

ASCENT/S USED

COMMENTS (walking companions, weather, etc.)

'Branstree is one of the very few Lakeland fells that have no view of lakes or tarns from the highest point, but Haweswater is brought into view by walking a few paces north. The long strip of water in the distance southwards is the Kent estuary.'

Brock Crags 1842'

from Goldrill Beck

• Patterdale
ANGLETARN ▲ PIKES
BROCK ▲ CRAGS
• Hartsop
HIGH STREET ▲
MILES
0 1 2 3 4

The unspoilt village of Low Hartsop has great charm and its environment is one of quiet loveliness, much of it contributed by the hanging woods of the steep fell that rises immediately behind. This fell, Brock Crags, is an offshoot of a ridge coming down to Ullswater from the main High Street watershed, and overlooks a meeting of many valleys: a feature in the view from the rocky top. Its slopes carry the Hayeswater aqueduct.

From Book Two

DATE/S WALKED

ASCENT/S USED

COMMENTS (walking companions, weather, etc.)

'The scene from the summit is interesting, with a fine surround of higher fells; in particular, the bird's-eye view of Brothers Water and Hartsop is beautiful and dramatic.'

Calf Crag 1762'

from the boulders below Deer Bield Crag

From Book Three

DATE/S WALKED

ASCENT/S USED

COMMENTS (walking companions, weather, etc.)

'The highest point, small and rocky, is a pleasant place for a halt and quiet contemplation of the scenery. Sheep think so, too, and wearers of new clothes should not sink into repose without first clearing away the profuse evidences of their occupation.'

Catstycam 2917'

sometimes called
Catchedicam

from Glenridding Beck

From Book One

DATE/S WALKED ....

....

....

ASCENT/S USED ....

....

....

COMMENTS (walking companions, weather, etc.) ....

....

....

....

....

....

....

....

....

....

....

....

....

'If Catstycam stood alone, remote from its fellows, it would be one of the finest peaks in Lakeland. It has nearly the perfect mountain form, and a small pointed top, a real summit that falls away sharply on all sides.'

Caudale Moor 2502'

often referred to as
John Bell's Banner
summit named
Stony Cove Pike

• Patterdale

• Hartsop

HIGH STREET ▲

CAUDALE ▲ MOOR

▲ RED SCREES

• Ambleside

MILES
0 1 2 3 4

from Brothers Water

From Book Two

DATE/S WALKED

ASCENT/S USED

COMMENTS (walking companions, weather, etc.)

'The beautiful retrospect over Patterdale is justification for frequent halts during the continuously steep ascent from Brothers Water. Of the many approaches to the summit, this is by far the best.'

Clough Head 2381'

from High Rigg

Threlkeld
Wanthwaite
▲ CLOUGH HEAD
▲ GREAT DODD
Legburthwaite
MILES
0 1 2 3

From Kirkstone Pass the massive main ridge of the Fairfield and Helvellyn fells runs north, mile after mile, throughout maintaining a consistently high and a remarkably uniform altitude, and with a dozen distinct summits over 2500'. At its northern extremity the ground falls away swiftly to the deep valley of the Glenderamackin, and the last outpost of the ridge, although not so elevated as the summits to the south, occupies a commanding site: this is Clough Head.

From Book One

DATE/S WALKED

ASCENT/S USED

COMMENTS (walking companions, weather, etc.)

'Clough Head is sufficiently isolated to afford an uninterrupted prospect in every direction except south-east. A special feature, rare in views from the heights of the Helvellyn range, is the nice combination of valley and mountain scenery.'

Dollywaggon Pike 2810'

From Book One

DATE/S WALKED

ASCENT/S USED

COMMENTS (walking companions, weather, etc.)

'Like most of the high fells south of the Sticks Pass, Dollywaggon Pike exhibits a marked contrast in its western and eastern aspects. The eastern side is a desolation of crag and boulder and scree: here are silent recesses rarely visited.'

Dove Crag 2603'

from Dovedale

Patterdale •

Hartsop •

▲ FAIRFIELD

DOVE ▲ CRAG

RED SCREES ▲

• Grasmere

Ambleside •

MILES

0 1 2 3 4

The lofty height that towers so magnificently over Dovedale is indebted for its name to a very impressive vertical wall of rock on its north-east flank: the crag was named first and the summit of the parent fell above, which officially is considered unworthy of any title and is nameless on the Ordnance Survey maps, has adopted it by common consent.

From Book One

DATE/S WALKED

ASCENT/S USED

COMMENTS (walking companions, weather, etc.)

'Dove Crag is most often ascended from Ambleside on the popular tour of the Fairfield Horseshoe – but the climb from Patterdale, by Dovedale, is far superior; it gives a much more interesting and intimate approach.'

Eagle Crag

1650' approx.

from Stonethwaite Beck

From Book Three

DATE/S WALKED

ASCENT/S USED

COMMENTS (walking companions, weather, etc.)

'Eagle Crag has a giant cornerstone so splendidly situated, so nobly proportioned and of so arresting an appearance that it is, to the eye of the artist and the mountaineer, a far worthier object than the parent fell rising behind.'

Fairfield

2863'

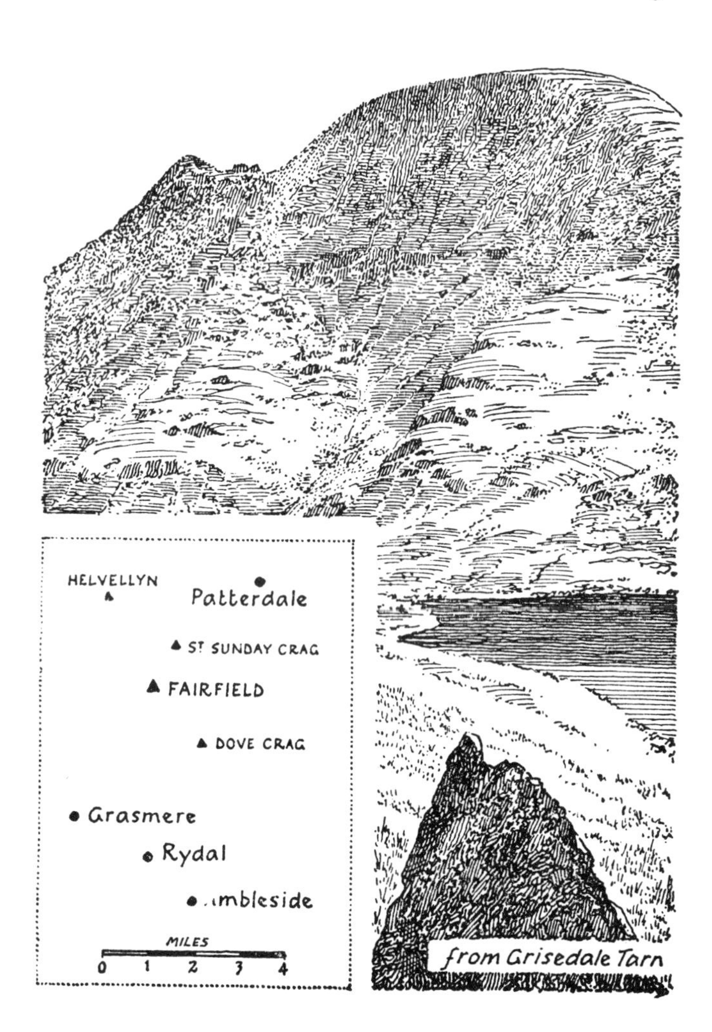

from Grisedale Tarn

From Book One

DATE/S WALKED

ASCENT/S USED

COMMENTS (walking companions, weather, etc.)

'The north side of the Fairfield range is magnificent: here are dark precipices, long fans of scree, abrupt crags, desolate combes and deep valleys: a tangle of rough country full of interest and well worth exploration.'

Froswick

2359'

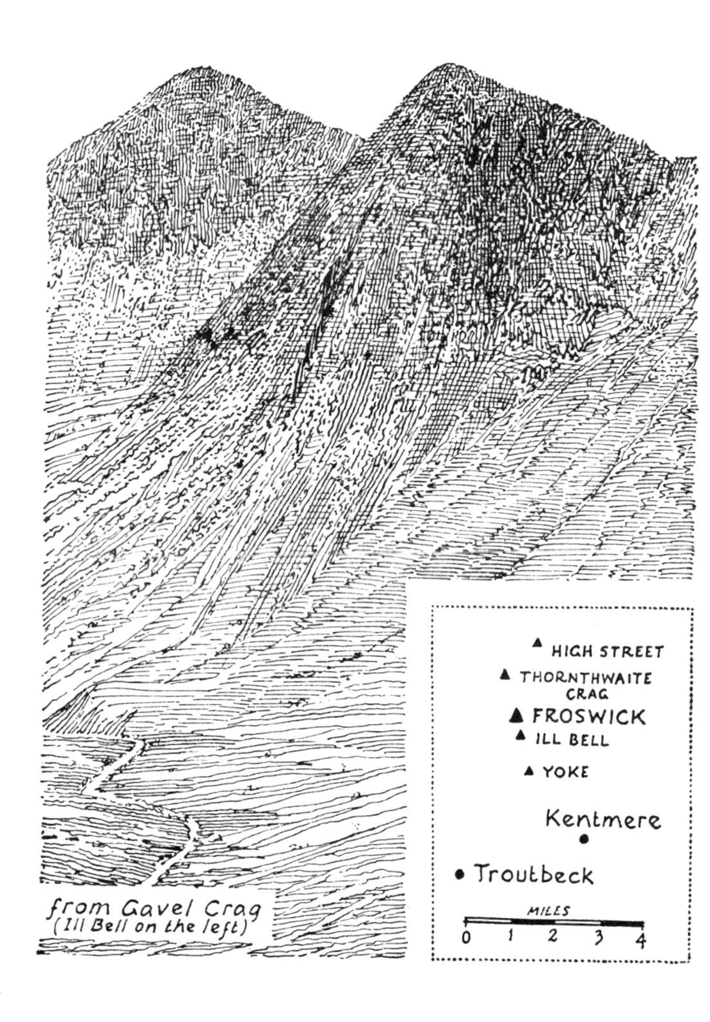

from Gavel Crag
(Ill Bell on the left)

From Book Two

DATE/S WALKED

ASCENT/S USED

COMMENTS (walking companions, weather, etc.)

'Sheltering in the shadow of Ill Bell on High Street's south ridge is the lesser height of Froswick. It takes its pattern from Ill Bell in remarkable degree, almost humorously seeming to ape its bigger neighbour.'

Gibson Knott 1379'

from Helm Crag

STEEL FELL
CALF CRAG
GIBSON KNOTT
HELM CRAG
Grasmere

MILES
0 1 2 3

Gibson Knott is the most elevated of the several sundry knobs and bumps that form the crest of the mile-long ridge linking at its extremities Calf Crag and Helm Crag and dividing the valleys of Far Easedale and Greenburn. There is much rock in evidence along the serrated top and fringing steep flanks; in particular, a prominent buttress, Horn Crag, adorned with juniper, rises from the bracken of the Easedale slope. The summit is interesting, other parts less so. The fellsides are 'dry', draining without forming regular watercourses.

From Book Three

DATE/S WALKED

ASCENT/S USED

COMMENTS (walking companions, weather, etc.)

'The cairn on the summit is not quite the best viewpoint: the ridge eastwards is more satisfying. There is strong contrast between the smooth slopes towering across the Keswick road and the rough territory and serrated skyline across Far Easedale.'

Glenridding Dodd

1425' approx.

from Ullswater
(Sheffield Pike behind)

Glencoyne •

GLENRIDDING DODD
▲

•
Glenridding

Patterdale •

MILES
0 1 2

Fashions change. When people climbed hills only for the sake of the views, the heathery summit of Glenridding Dodd must have been more frequented than it is today, for once-popular paths of ascent are now overgrown and neglected. It occupies a grand position overlooking the upper reach of Ullswater. It is the end, topographically, of the eastern shoulder of Stybarrow Dodd.

From Book One

DATE/S WALKED ....

....

....

ASCENT/S USED ....

....

....

COMMENTS (walking companions, weather, etc.) ....

....

....

....

....

....

....

....

....

....

....

....

....

....

'On a sunny day in August the summit is a delectable place. It is richly clothed with heather, and larches almost reach the top of the north side.'

Since A. Wainwright wrote the facing text, this fell has regained its popularity.

Gowbarrow Fell 1579'

From Book One

DATE/S WALKED ....

....

....

ASCENT/S USED ....

....

....

COMMENTS (walking companions, weather, etc.) ....

....

....

....

....

....

....

....

....

....

....

....

....

....

'Gowbarrow Fell is one of the best known of Lakeland's lesser heights, much of it being National Trust property, and a favourite playground and picnic-place. It is not the fell itself that brings the crowds, however: the great attraction is Aira Force.'

Grange Fell 1363'

King's How, from Shepherds Crag

Grange Fell is nothing on the map, everything when beneath one's feet. In small compass, here is concentrated the beauty, romance, interest and excitement of the typical Lakeland scene. Here Nature has given of her very best and produced a loveliness that is exquisite. Not strictly the territory of fellwalkers, perhaps; yet those who consistently hurry past Grange Fell to get to grips with the Scafells and Gable would do well to turn aside to it once in a while, alone, and quietly walk its sylvan glades and heathery top. The exercise will not tire the limbs, but it will do the heart and spirit and faith of the walker a power of good, and gladden his eye exceedingly.

Rising abruptly between Borrowdale and Watendlath Beck, and split by that delightful little valley of trees, Troutdale, the fell is almost encircled by a grey girdle of crags half-hidden in rich foliage; below is the wreckage of centuries in the form of masses of boulders (one of which, the Bowder Stone, is famous) overgrown by lush bracken and screened by a forest of birches. The top of the fell is an up-and-down tangled plateau, from which rise three main summits: (1) Brund Fell, the highest; (2) King's How, deservedly the best-known; and (3) Ether Knott behind a barricade of long heather.

Lodore
HIGH SEAT
Grange
GRANGE FELL
Watendlath
Rosthwaite
MILES
0 1 2 3

From Book Three

DATE/S WALKED ....

....

....

ASCENT/S USED ....

....

....

COMMENTS (walking companions, weather, etc.) ....

....

....

....

....

....

....

....

....

....

....

....

....

....

'The ascent of Grange Fell from Grange is a most beautifu short climb. The first part, to King's How, is exquisitel lovely (in autumn, a golden ladder to heaven) and simpl must not be missed. Sacrifice any other walk, if need be but not this!'

Gray Crag 2286'

from Hartsop

From Book Two

DATE/S WALKED

ASCENT/S USED

COMMENTS (walking companions, weather, etc.)

'A lofty ridge, bounded by exceedingly steep flanks, extends northwards from Thornthwaite Crag with a slight curve to the west, and culminates high above Hayeswater Gill in a level platform from which, on both sides, fall precipitous crags split by deep gullies. This is Gray Crag.'

Great Crag

1500′ approx.

Between the deep Stonethwaite valley and the shallow depression containing Bleatarn Gill rises an indefinite and complex mass of rough undulating ground, a place of craggy and wooded slopes, of heathery tors and mossy swamps and shy little tarns — a beautiful labyrinth, a joy to the explorer but the despair of the map-maker. Nestling here is Dock Tarn, a jewel deserving a sweeter name, in a surround of rocky heights of which Great Crag is the most pronounced, and the natural summit of the fell — although perhaps not quite the highest point. Its altitude is not given on Ordnance maps, nor a 1500′ contour, but the cairn can be little below this height, if at all.

Great Crag is one of those modest fells which seldom seem to invite attention, and few people know it by name, yet many are they who have trodden its lower slopes on the popular path of the pilgrims journeying to Watendlath from Rosthwaite.

Lakeland is not usually associated with heather — but here it thrives with a tropical vigour, and walking in it is arduous and difficult.

From Book Three

DATE/S WALKED

ASCENT/S USED

COMMENTS (walking companions, weather, etc.)

'On the right sort of day (warm sunshine) and at the right time of year (August) the top of Great Crag, carpeted with lovely heather, is quite the right place to be. Nearby, Dock Tarn is a place to lie adreaming, and life seems a sweet, sweet thing.'

Great Dodd
2807'
Threlkeld
CLOUGH HEAD
Dockray
Fornside
GREAT DODD
Legburthwaite
STYBARROW DODD
RAISE
Glenridding
HELVELLYN
MILES
0 1 2 3 4
from High Rigg

From Book One

DATE/S WALKED

ASCENT/S USED

COMMENTS (walking companions, weather, etc.)

'To the north-east of Great Dodd, long sprawling slopes fall away gradually in an undulating wilderness of grass to the old coach-road; beyond is a wide expanse of uncultivated marshland. It seems an oversight of nature that the sheep here are not born with webbed feet.'

Great Mell Fell 1760'

from Great Meldrum

Troutbeck
Penruddock
GREAT ▲ MELL FELL
▲ LITTLE MELL FELL
Matterdale End
▲ GOWBARROW FELL
Dockray
MILES
0 1 2 3 4

Great Mell Fell is a prominent object on the Penrith approach to Lakeland. With its lesser twin, Little Mell Fell, it forms the portals to the Helvellyn range on this side. Its round 'inverted pudding-basin' shape does not promise much for the walker and it is rarely climbed. On closer acquaintance, however, it is rather more enjoyable than its appearance suggests, because of the presence of fine woodlands on the lower slopes; indeed pines and larches persist almost to the summit.

From Book One

DATE/S WALKED

ASCENT/S USED

COMMENTS (walking companions, weather, etc.)

'Great Mell Fell rises sharply from a wide expanse of desolate marshland, territory not at all typical of Lakeland, the fell itself being much more fertile and colourful than its surroundings.'

Great Rigg 2513'

from Grasmere

From Book One

DATE/S WALKED

ASCENT/S USED

COMMENTS (walking companions, weather, etc.)

'Few people will climb Great Rigg without also ascending Fairfield, for the former is a stepping stone to its bigger neighbour. Whilst providing this humble service, however, the fell manages to retain a certain dignity.'

Grey Crag
2093'
HARTER FELL
TARN CRAG
KENTMERE PIKE
GREY CRAG
road summit
Longsleddale
Hucks Bridge
Jungle Café
Selside
Garnett Bridge
MILES
0 1 2 3 4 5
from Shipman Knotts

From Book Two

DATE/S WALKED ....

....

....

ASCENT/S USED ....

....

....

COMMENTS (walking companions, weather, etc.) ....

....

....

....

....

....

....

....

....

....

....

....

....

....

'There is nothing remarkable about Grey Crag, but here Lakeland may be said to start and moorland country to end – and the transition is sudden: the quiet beauty gives place to romantic beauty, placid scenery to exciting. One looks east, and the heart is soothed; west, and it is stirred.'

Hallin Fell 1271'

from above Mellguards

Hallin Fell, beautifully situated overlooking a curve of Ullswater and commanding unrivalled views of the lovely secluded hinterland of Martindale, may be regarded as the motorists' fell, for the sandals and slippers and polished shoes of the numerous car-owners who park their properties on the crest of the road above the Howtown zig-zags on Sunday afternoons have smoothed to its summit a wide track that is seldom violated by the hobnails of fellwalkers. In choosing Hallin Fell as their weekend picnic-place and playground the Penrith and Carlisle motorists show commendable discrimination, for the rich rewards its summit offers are out of all proportion to the slight effort of ascent.

HALLIN FELL
Sandwick Howtown
PLACE FELL
BEDA FELL
Patterdale
MILES
0 1 2 3

From Book Two

DATE/S WALKED

ASCENT/S USED

COMMENTS (walking companions, weather, etc.)

'The man who built the summit-cairn did more than indicate the highest point: he erected for himself a permanent memorial. This 12-foot obelisk, a landmark for miles around, is a massive structure of squared and prepared stone.'

Harrison Stickle 2403'

the highest of the Langdale Pikes

from Great Langdale Beck

From Book Three

DATE/S WALKED ....

....

....

ASCENT/S USED ....

....

....

COMMENTS (walking companions, weather, etc.) ....

....

....

....

....

....

....

....

....

....

....

....

....

....

'The uninitiated climber who scales Harrison Stickle from Langdale expecting to find the northerly slopes descending as steeply as those he has just ascended will be surprised to see, on reaching the main cairn, that higher ground continues beyond a very shallow depression.'

Hart Crag 2698'

from Dovedale

From Book One

DATE/S WALKED

ASCENT/S USED

COMMENTS (walking companions, weather, etc.)

'The ascent from Patterdale is far superior to that from Rydal in the south. The Link Cove route especially is an interesting climb through the inner sanctuary of Hart Crag, the scene being impressive.'

Harter Fell

2539'

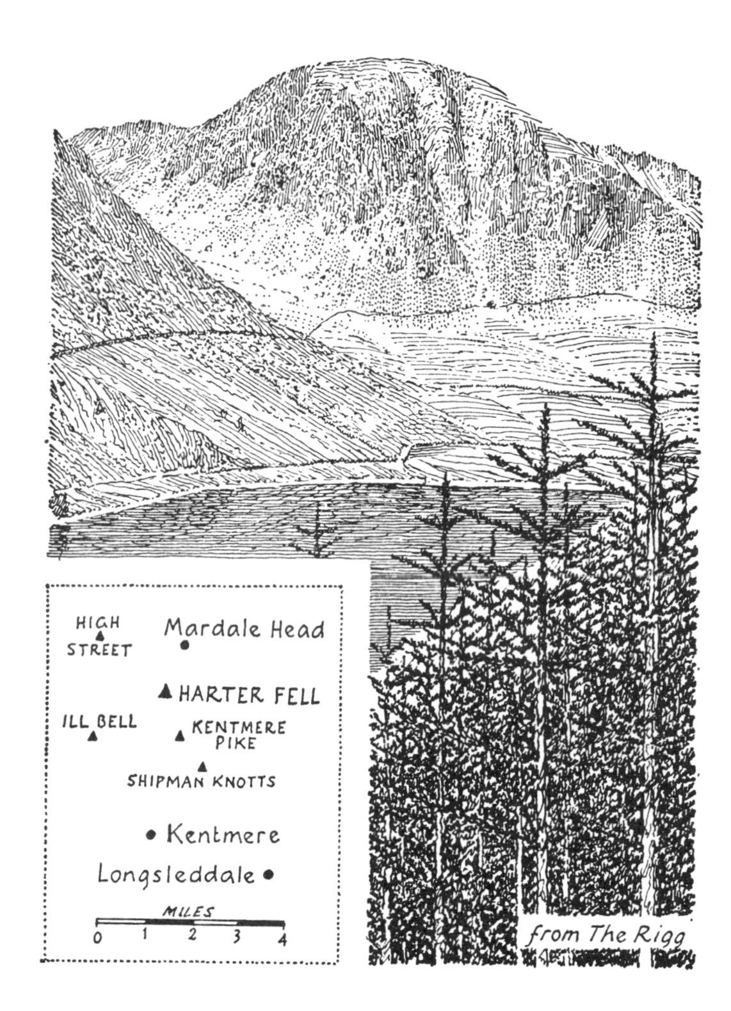

From Book Two

DATE/S WALKED ....

....

....

ASCENT/S USED ....

....

....

COMMENTS (walking companions, weather, etc.) ....

....

....

....

....

....

....

....

....

....

....

....

....

....

'Here a shelf cradles Small Water, which is the finest of Lakeland's tarns in the opinion of many qualified to judge: seen in storm, the picture is most impressive and awe-inspiring.'

Hart Side 2481'

From Book One

DATE/S WALKED ....

....

....

ASCENT/S USED ....

....

....

COMMENTS (walking companions, weather, etc.) ....

....

....

....

....

....

....

....

....

....

....

....

....

....

'Hart Side is rarely visited. Its smooth slopes, grass and marsh intermingling, seem very very remote from industry, but there are evidences that men laboured on these lonely heights a long time ago.'

Hartsop above How 1870'

from Hunsett Cove

Patterdale
ST SUNDAY CRAG
Hartsop
FAIRFIELD
HARTSOP ABOVE HOW
HART CRAG
DOVE CRAG
MILES
0 1 2 3

The long curving northeast ridge of Hart Crag rises to a separate summit midway, and this summit is generally referred to as Hartsop above How by guidebook writers and mapmakers. Sometimes the three words in the name are hyphenated, sometimes not. Probably the first two should be, but not the last two: the word 'How' is common, meaning a low hill, and the distinctive title of this particular How is 'Hartsop-above,' indicating its geographical relationship to the hamlet in the valley below. Most natives of Deepdale, however, know it not by this name, with or without hyphens, but they all know Gill Crag, which fringes the summit, and this would seem to be a more satisfactory name for the fell. But one cannot so wantonly ignore the authority of the guidebooks and maps; and the name Hartsop above How, without hyphens (in the belief that an error of omission is a less sin than an error of commission) will be used here in support of the Director General of Ordnance Survey.

From Book One

DATE/S WALKED

ASCENT/S USED

COMMENTS (walking companions, weather, etc.)

'Hartsop above How is a simple ridge curving like a sickle to enclose the valley of Deepdale on the south and east. The slopes above Brothers Water are well-wooded over an extensive area, and Deepdale Park also has some fine trees.'

Hartsop Dodd 2018'

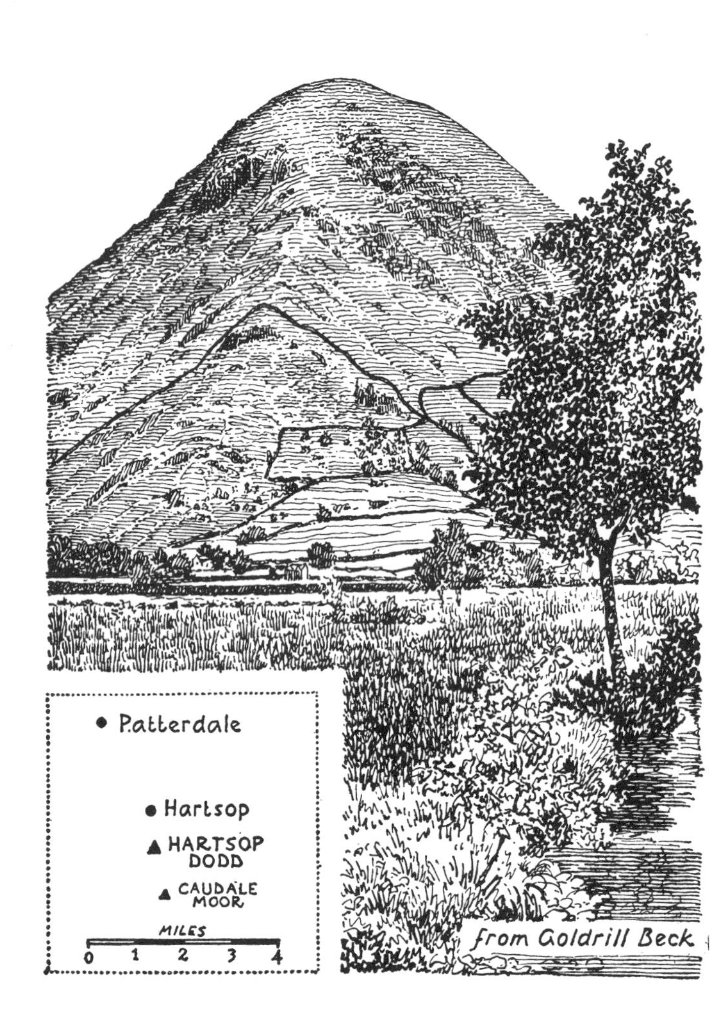

from Goldrill Beck

From Book Two

DATE/S WALKED ....

....

....

ASCENT/S USED ....

....

....

COMMENTS (walking companions, weather, etc.) ....

....

....

....

....

....

....

....

....

....

....

....

....

....

'Hartsop Dodd rises from pleasant places, pastures and woods and water, and quite rightly has been named from the delightful hamlet nestling unspoilt among trees at its foot. The view of Dove Crag and Dovedale across the gulf of Patterdale valley from the summit is a classic amongst views.'

Helm Crag 1299'

affectionately known as 'The Lion and The Lamb'

This is the smallest (and most accurate!) map in the book

From Book Three

DATE/S WALKED

ASCENT/S USED

COMMENTS (walking companions, weather, etc.)

'Helm Crag may well be the best-known of all Lakeland fells and its virtues have not been lauded enough. It gives an exhilarating little climb, a brief essay in real mountaineering, and, in a region where all is beautiful, it makes a notable contribution.'

Helvellyn 3118'

from the south-west ridge of St Sunday Crag

From Book One

DATE/S WALKED

ASCENT/S USED

COMMENTS (walking companions, weather, etc.)

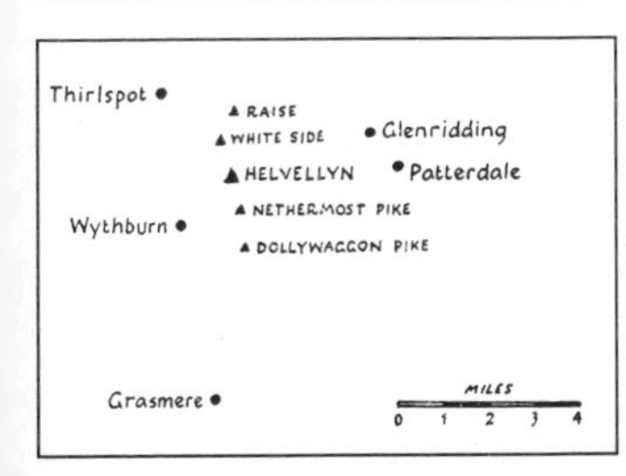

'Legend and poetry, a lovely name and a lofty altitude combine to encompass Helvellyn in an aura of romance; and thousands of pilgrims are attracted to its summit every year.'

Heron Pike 2003'

Heron Pike is a grassy mound on the long southern ridge of Fairfield. From no direction does it look like a pike or peak nor will herons be found there. It is a viewpoint of some merit but otherwise is of little interest. It is climbed not, as a rule, for any attraction of its own, but because it happens to lie on a popular route to Fairfield. The ridge beyond it undulates with little change of altitude before rising sharply to Great Rigg, and this hinterland of Heron Pike is generally referred to as Rydal Fell : for convenience it will be described in this chapter as a part of Heron Pike.

From Book One

DATE/S WALKED ....

....

....

ASCENT/S USED ....

....

....

COMMENTS (walking companions, weather, etc.) ....

....

....

....

....

....

....

....

....

....

....

....

....

'The smallness of the summit gives depth to the views, which are particularly rich in lakes and tarns. Nearby are the fells of the Fairfield Horseshoe, but the best of the mountain scene is formed by the finely-grouped Coniston and Langdale fells with Scafell Pike overtopping all.'

High Hartsop Dodd 1702'

from Hartsop Beck

Patterdale
Hartsop
Hartsop Hall
DOVE CRAG
HIGH HARTSOP DODD
LITTLE HART CRAG
RED SCREES
MILES
0 1 2 3

High Hartsop Dodd, seen from the valley near Brothers Water, has the appearance of an isolated mountain with a peaked summit and steep sides, a very shapely pyramid rising from green fields. But in fact it is merely the termination of a spur of a higher fell, Little Hart Crag, which it partly hides from view, and its uninteresting grassy summit has little distinction, though it is always greeted with enthusiasm by walkers who attain it direct from the valley, for the upper slopes above the sparsely-wooded lower flanks are excessively steep. A high ascending ridge links the Dodd with the rough top of Little Hart Crag.

From Book One

DATE/S WALKED ....

....

....

ASCENT/S USED ....

....

....

COMMENTS (walking companions, weather, etc.) ....

....

....

....

....

....

....

....

....

....

....

....

....

....

....

'The most striking feature in a moderate view from the summit is the exceptionally fine picture of Dovedale, which is seen intimately in all its strong and impressive contrasts.'

High Pike 2155'

sometimes referred to as
Scandale Fell

from High Sweden Bridge

▲ DOVE CRAG

▲ HIGH PIKE

▲ LOW PIKE

• Rydal

• Ambleside

MILES
0 1 2 3

Everest enthusiasts will liken the two pronounced rises on the long southern spur of Dove Crag to the 'first and second steps' on the famous north-east ridge (but imagination would indeed have to be vivid to see in the grassy dome of Dove Crag any resemblance to the icy pyramid of that highest of all peaks!). The first rise is Low Pike, the second is High Pike. The latter, with its cairn perched on the brink of a shattered cliff, is the most imposing object seen from Scandale which lies far below.

Some authorities refer to High Pike as Scandale Fell, but the latter name is more properly applied in a general way to the whole of the high ground enclosing Scandale Bottom to north and west.

From Book One

DATE/S WALKED

ASCENT/S USED

COMMENTS (walking companions, weather, etc.)

'The ascent from Ambleside, commonly used as the initial stage of the Fairfield Horseshoe, provides a pleasant walk along a good ridge. The lower approaches are very attractive.'

High Raise 2634'

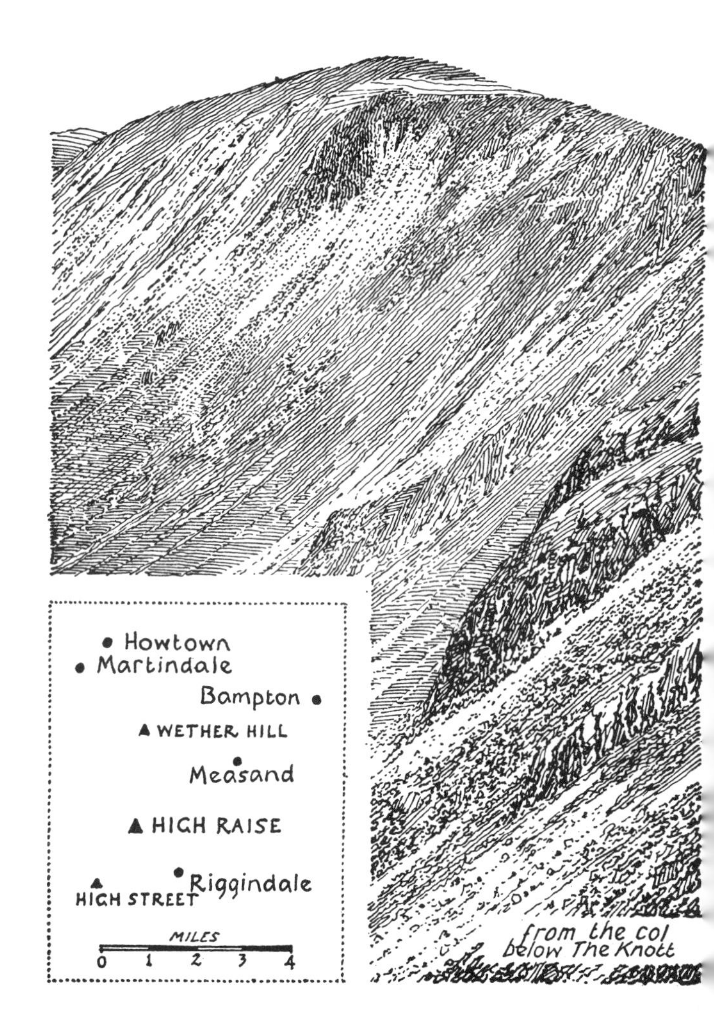

from the col below The Knott

From Book Two

DATE/S WALKED

ASCENT/S USED

COMMENTS (walking companions, weather, etc.)

'Second in altitude among the fells east of Kirkstone and Ullswater, High Raise is overtopped only by High Street itself. Its summit-cone rises distinctively from the lofty watershed of the main range, and it is the last fell, going north, with the characteristics of a mountain.'

High Raise 2500'

summit named
High White Stones

From Book Three

DATE/S WALKED ....

....

....

ASCENT/S USED ....

....

....

COMMENTS (walking companions, weather, etc.) ....

....

....

....

....

....

....

....

....

....

....

....

....

....

Stonethwaite
Wythburn
ULLSCARF
HIGH RAISE
SERGEANT MAN
HARRISON STICKLE
MILES
0 1 2 3 4
Grasmere
New Hotel
Old Hotel
Dungeon Ghyll

'High Raise occupies a magnificent position geographically, many valleys radiating from the wide upper slopes.'

High Rigg 1163'

from Sosgill Bridge

The valley running north from Dunmail Raise, and containing Thirlmere, is suddenly confronted by a steep, abrupt fell just at that final stage in its course when, with the highest hills left behind, it might reasonably be expected to go on more leisurely, as is the fashion with valleys born among mountains. Escape is found in a narrow ravine to the right, which opens out into St. John's-in-the-Vale; and, because this intrusive fell stands in isolation from other high ground, a subsidiary valley, that of Naddle Beck, forms at the base of the left flank. The waters mingle only when the River Greta is joined four miles to the north. This isolated wedge is High Rigg (locally known as Naddle Fell): it is rough and craggy although of modest elevation only. Northwards the ridge falls to a pass, where there is a Church, so sited to serve both valleys equally (and an object of pilgrimage for many visitors to Keswick), beyond which rises Low Rigg, merely a rough pasture, followed by an easy slope descending to Tewet Tarn and the Keswick - Penrith road.

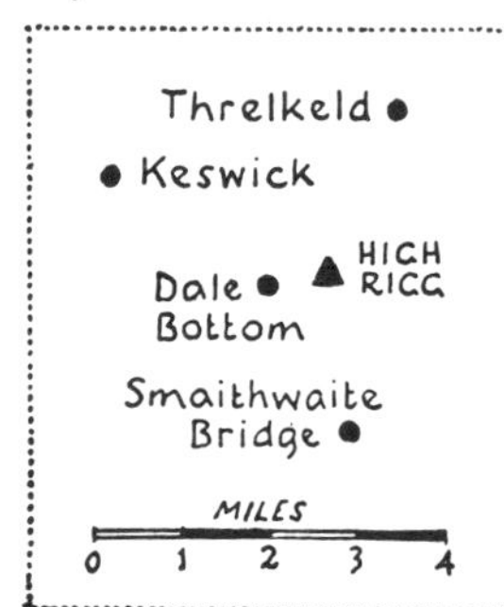

From Book Three

DATE/S WALKED

ASCENT/S USED

COMMENTS (walking companions, weather, etc.)

'The cairn stands on a small rocky knoll, easily identifiable although not appreciably higher than some other parts of the fell. The view is interesting, with Blencathra especially well displayed, and Clough Head very impressive.'

High Seat 1995'

from Fisher Crag

● Keswick

● Dale Bottom

▲ BLEABERRY FELL

● Lodore

▲ HIGH SEAT

● Armboth

▲ HIGH TOVE

● Watendlath

● Rosthwaite

MILES

0 1 2 3 4

Reecastle Crag

From Book Three

DATE/S WALKED ....

....

....

ASCENT/S USED ....

....

....

COMMENTS (walking companions, weather, etc.) ....

....

....

....

....

....

....

....

....

....

....

....

....

....

'High Seat is the principal fell on the north section of the central ridge, overtopping all others within a radius of some miles. It is therefore a first-class viewpoint, with much of interest to see in all directions.'

High Street 2718'

from the north ridge of Branstree

From Book Two

DATE/S WALKED ....

....

....

ASCENT/S USED ....

....

....

COMMENTS (walking companions, weather, etc.) ....

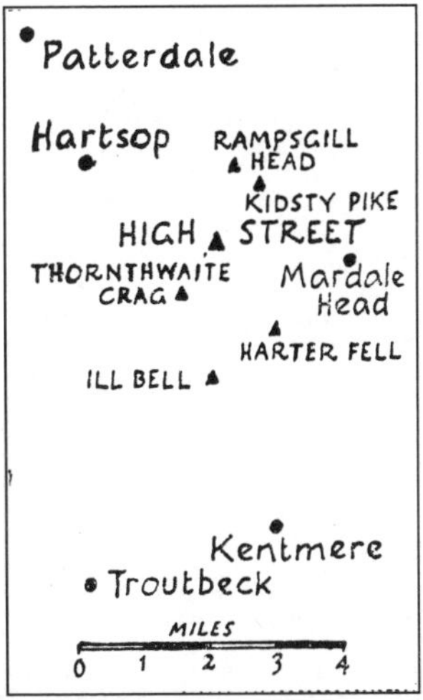

....

....

....

....

....

....

....

....

....

....

....

....

'The summit of High Street has been in turn a highway and a sports arena and a racecourse, as well as, as it is today, a grazing ground for sheep.'

High Tove 1665'

from Armboth Fell

It is hard to imagine that anybody feels any affection at all for High Tove, apart perhaps from the sheep whose natural heaf it is. This dark heathery mound, squatting on the ridge between Watendlath and Thirlmere, and so gently contoured that water cannot drain away from it, is everywhere shockingly wet — a condition persisting even in drought — and is without any redeeming feature except as a viewpoint. Yet it is climbed a thousand times every year, probably, and maybe more: the explanation is that High Tove is crossed by a public and fairly well used footpath that gives the shortest route across the central ridge. In fact, in this respect High Tove is unique, for where else is a summit used as a pass? This oddity arises because the depressions on either side are not only insignificant but even wetter than the way over the top.

A geographical curiosity is the twist in the indefinite north-east ridge, which, after ambling down easily towards, apparently, the obvious destination of Thirlmere, unexpectedly changes character and rises again as a high rocky rampart now heading due north in a heavy screen of trees to the abrupt, exciting top of Raven Crag

HIGH SEAT
Armboth
HIGH TOVE
Watendlath
Rosthwaite
Wythburn
ULLSCARF
MILES
0 1 2 3 4

From Book Three

DATE/S WALKED

ASCENT/S USED

COMMENTS (walking companions, weather, etc.)

'The top has pretensions to beauty only when the heather is in bloom; for most of the year it is a dreary place. A big cairn offers a seat to travellers to pour the water out of their boots.'

Ill Bell   2476'

From Book Two

DATE/S WALKED

ASCENT/S USED

COMMENTS (walking companions, weather, etc.)

'The graceful cone of Ill Bell is a familiar object to most residents of south Westmorland and those visitors who approach Lakeland by way of Kendal and Windermere, although few who know it by sight can give it a name and fewer still its correct name.'

Kentmere Pike 2397'

from Ill Bell (north-east ridge)

From Book Two

DATE/S WALKED ....

....

....

ASCENT/S USED ....

....

....

COMMENTS (walking companions, weather, etc.) ....

....

....

....

....

....

....

....

....

....

....

....

....

....

'The eastern flank falls precipitously into the narrow jaws of Longsleddale: a most impressive scene. Here, abrupt cliffs riven by deep gullies tower high above the crystal waters of the winding Sprint.'

Kidsty Pike 2560'

from Twopenny Crag

From Book Two

DATE/S WALKED ....

....

....

ASCENT/S USED ....

....

....

COMMENTS (walking companions, weather, etc.) ....

....

....

....

....

....

....

....

....

....

....

....

....

'The summit is an eyrie perched high above Riggindale. The small cairn stands on grass amongst the boulders of the top pedestal, and crags are immediately below. The situation is dramatic. The summit is the best feature of the fell.'

The Knott

2423'

from Hayeswater Gill

From Book Two

DATE/S WALKED

ASCENT/S USED

COMMENTS (walking companions, weather, etc.)

'The steep western slope descending from Rampsgill Head is arrested below the summit, just as the fall is gathering impetus, by a protuberance that takes the shape of a small conical hill. This is the Knott.'

Little Hart Crag 2091'

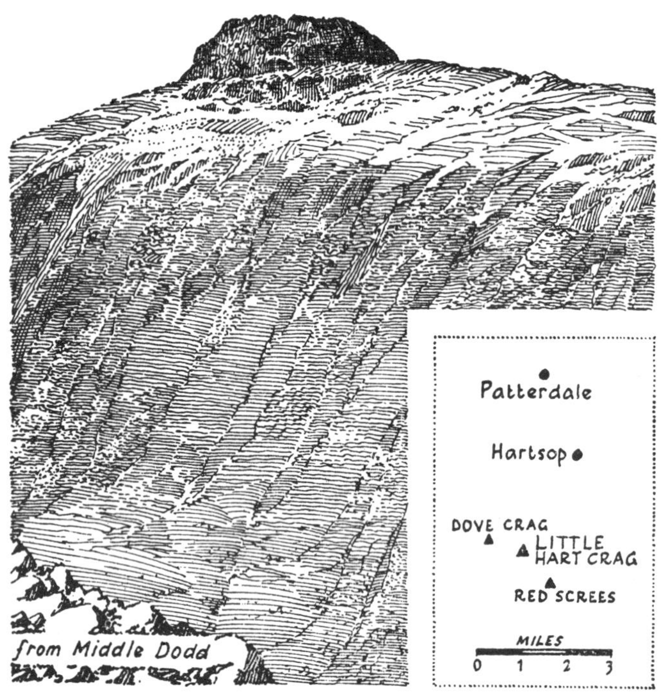

Little Hart Crag is the sentinel of Scandale Pass, four miles north of Ambleside, and takes its duty of guarding the Pass very seriously and proudly. It has the appearance, in fact, of a crouching watchdog, facing Scandale and missing nothing of the happenings there, while its spine curves down to the fields of Hartsop; the path from one place to the other climbs over its shoulder just beneath the hoary head and beetling brows.

It is really a very junior member in a company of grand hills and quite overshadowed by Red Screes and Dove Crag; but it has individuality and an interesting double summit which commands delightful views of Scandale and Dovedale.

From Book One

DATE/S WALKED ....

....

....

ASCENT/S USED ....

....

....

COMMENTS (walking companions, weather, etc.) ....

....

....

....

....

....

....

....

....

....

....

....

....

....

'There are two well-defined tops. The higher is that nearer to Dove Crag; it is surmounted by a cairn perched on the extreme edge of a rocky platform. The lower summit is easily identified in mist by markings of quartz in the stones near the insignificant cairn.'

Little Mell Fell 1657'

from Gowbarrow Fell

Little Mell Fell barely merits inclusion in this book. It *is* a fell – its name says so – but it is not the stuff of which the true fells are made. It rises on the verge of Lakeland but its characteristics are alien to Lakeland. It stands in isolation, not in the company of others. Its substance looks more akin to the sandstones of the nearby valley of Eden; its patchwork clothing, gorse and ling prominent, is unusual on the other fells; its hedges of stunted, windblown, unhappy trees and tumbledown fences are unsatisfactory substitutes for friendly stone walls. It is ringed by a quiet and pleasant countryside of green pastures and lush hedgerows, and one is as likely to meet a cow as a sheep on its slopes. There is good in all, however, and its heathery top is a fine place for viewing the (greater) merits of other fells.

Penruddock
GREAT MELL FELL
LITTLE MELL FELL
Pooley Bridge
Watermillock
GOWBARROW FELL
Dockray
MILES
0 1 2 3 4

From Book One

DATE/S WALKED ....

....

....

ASCENT/S USED ....

....

....

COMMENTS (walking companions, weather, etc.) ....

....

....

....

....

....

....

....

....

....

....

....

....

....

'One feels sorry for Little Mell Fell, as for all who are neglected and forlorn, but at least it is beloved of birds and animals and it is one of the few fells that grouse select for their habitat, and not even the great Helvellyn itself can make such a claim!'

Loadpot Hill 2201'

from Sandwick

• Pooley Bridge
• Askham
Helton •
▲ ARTHUR'S PIKE
• Howtown
▲ LOADPOT HILL
• Bampton
▲ WETHER HILL

MILES
0 1 2 3 4

The beacon on The Pen

From Book Two

DATE/S WALKED ....

....

....

ASCENT/S USED ....

....

....

COMMENTS (walking companions, weather, etc.) ....

....

....

....

....

....

....

....

....

....

....

....

....

....

'Loadpot Hill is a natural sanctuary for all wild life. Hardy fell ponies roam and graze at will, and the Martindale deer often cross the watershed; in springtime especially, the number and variety of birds is quite unusual for the fells.'

Loft Crag

2270' approx.

the third of the Langdale Pikes

from Pike o' Stickle

The Langdale Pikes are variously regarded as being from two to five in number. Thorn Crag and Pavey Ark, often included in the count, have not the distinctive outline of the others, and should perhaps more properly be omitted, but Loft Crag most certainly has the qualifying characteristics. It lies between Pike o' Stickle and Harrison Stickle but south of them, having a small, abrupt summit (often mistaken for Pike o' Stickle in views from the east) directly below which is the magnificent buttress of Gimmer Crag, most popular of all climbing-grounds. Beyond Thorn Crag, a subsidiary summit, the deep-cut ravines of Dungeon Ghyll form the eastern boundary of the fell, but on the west side the line of demarcation is less exact, watercourses being submerged in rivers of scree. The short north slopes, after initial rocks, are soon lost in the wide depression of Harrison Combe.

Although it must rank after the two Stickles, Loft Crag is a worthy member of a fine trinity of peaks.

From Book Three

DATE/S WALKED

ASCENT/S USED

COMMENTS (walking companions, weather, etc.)

'The small, delicately-poised summit makes a splendid halting-place, both for a survey of the fells around the head of Langdale, and for its own comfortable bilberry couches, whether fruit-bearing or not.'

Loughrigg Fell 1101'

more often referred to simply as 'Loughrigg' *(pronounced Luffrigg)*

Grasmere
SILVER HOW
Rydal
LOUGHRIGG FELL
Ambleside
Clappersgate
Skelwith Bridge
MILES
0 1 2 3 4

from Mandale Bridge (near Skelwith Bridge)

From Book Three

DATE/S WALKED

ASCENT/S USED

COMMENTS (walking companions, weather, etc.)

'Loughrigg has delightful grassy paths, several charming vistas and magnificent views, fine contrasts of velvety turf, rich bracken and grey rock, a string of little tarns like pearls in a necklace, and a wealth of stately trees on the flanks.'

Low Pike 1657'

from Rydal Beck

▲ HIGH PIKE

▲ LOW PIKE

● Rydal

● Ambleside

MILES
0 1 2 3

Low Pike is well seen from the streets of Ambleside as the first prominent peak on the high ridge running northwards. The gradient along the crest of the ridge is slight, but Low Pike, halfway along, is sufficiently elevated above the deep valleys of Scandale, east, and Rydale, west, to give an impression of loftiness which exaggerates its modest altitude. There is a good deal of rock on the fell with several tiers of low crag. Low Pike is the objective in the fell-races at the annual sports meetings in Rydal Park.

From Book One

DATE/S WALKED

ASCENT/S USED

COMMENTS (walking companions, weather, etc.)

'Low Pike is invariably climbed from Ambleside, usually on the way to the high fells beyond; it is, however, an excellent objective for a short walk from that town. The approach from the pleasant woods and pastures to the bleak craggy ridge is very attractive.'

Mardale Ill Bell 2496'

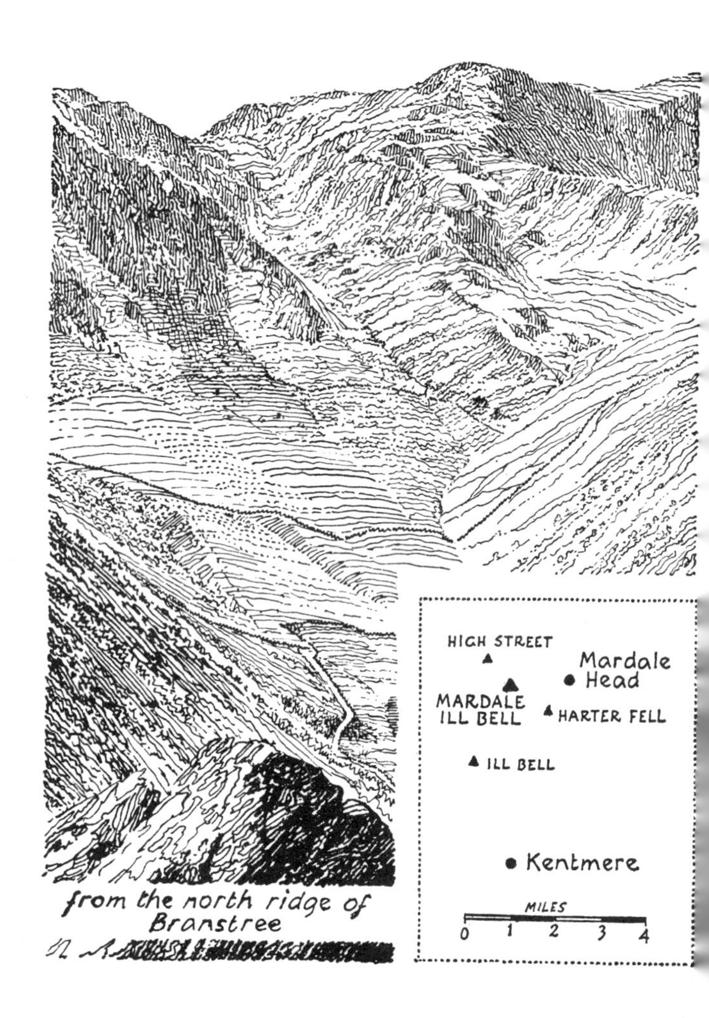

from the north ridge of Branstree

From Book Two

DATE/S WALKED ....

....

....

ASCENT/S USED ....

....

....

COMMENTS (walking companions, weather, etc.) ....

....

....

....

....

....

....

....

....

....

....

....

....

....

'Of the many excellent climbs available from Mardale Head the direct ascent of Mardale Ill Bell ranks high, the walk being favoured by striking views of two of the finest tarns in Lakeland, each set amongst crags in wild and romantic surroundings.'

Middle Dodd 2106'

Patterdale
Hartsop
Hartsop Hall
DOVE CRAG
MIDDLE DODD
RED SCREES
MILES
0 1 2 3

To the traveller starting the long climb up to Kirkstone Pass from Brothers Water the most striking object in a fine array of mountain scenery is the steep pyramid ahead: it towers high above the road like a gigantic upturned boat, its keel touching the sky, its sides barnacled and hoary. This pyramid is Middle Dodd, the middle one of three dodds which rise from the pastures of Hartsop, all exhibiting the same characteristics. When seen from higher ground in the vicinity, however, Middle Dodd loses its regal appearance (as do the other two); its summit then is obviously nothing more than a halt in the long northern spur of Red Screes.

From Book One

DATE/S WALKED ....

....

....

ASCENT/S USED ....

....

....

COMMENTS (walking companions, weather, etc.) ....

....

....

....

....

....

....

....

....

....

....

....

....

'Near the cairn is a series of curious depressions like a line of sinkholes in limestone country, but as the rock here is volcanic the probability is that they are old earthworks. Walkers who are neither archaeologists nor geologists will see in the depressions only a refuge from the wind.'

Nab Scar

1450′
approx.

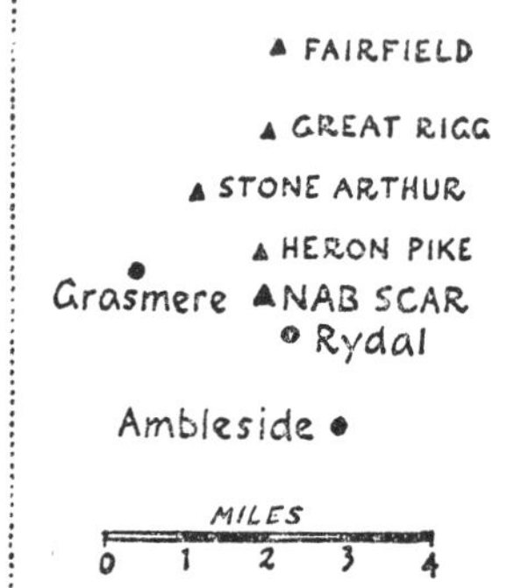

from Rydal Water

From Book One

DATE/S WALKED ....

....

....

ASCENT/S USED ....

....

....

COMMENTS (walking companions, weather, etc.) ....

....

....

....

....

....

....

....

....

....

....

....

....

'Nab Scar is well known. Its associations with the Lake Poets who came to dwell at the foot of its steep wooded slopes have invested it with romance, and its commanding position overlooking Rydal Water brings it to the notice of the many visitors to that charming lake.'

The Nab

1887'

from Rampsgill Beck

The Nab is situated wholly within the Martindale Deer Forest. The boundaries of the Forest are principally defined by the 'Forest Wall,' which encloses much of the Rampsgill and Bannerdale valleys and crosses the high ground between. This wall does not confine the deer — they roam freely beyond the boundaries — but it marks their home, their only safe refuge, their one sanctuary.

PLEASE DO NOT INTRUDE.

Red Deer Stag

Please note that because of the Martindale Deer Forest (see opposite), there is no right of way on to The Nab. The three paths shown on the 2½″ Ordnance Survey Map are private stalkers' paths.

Nethermost Pike 2920'

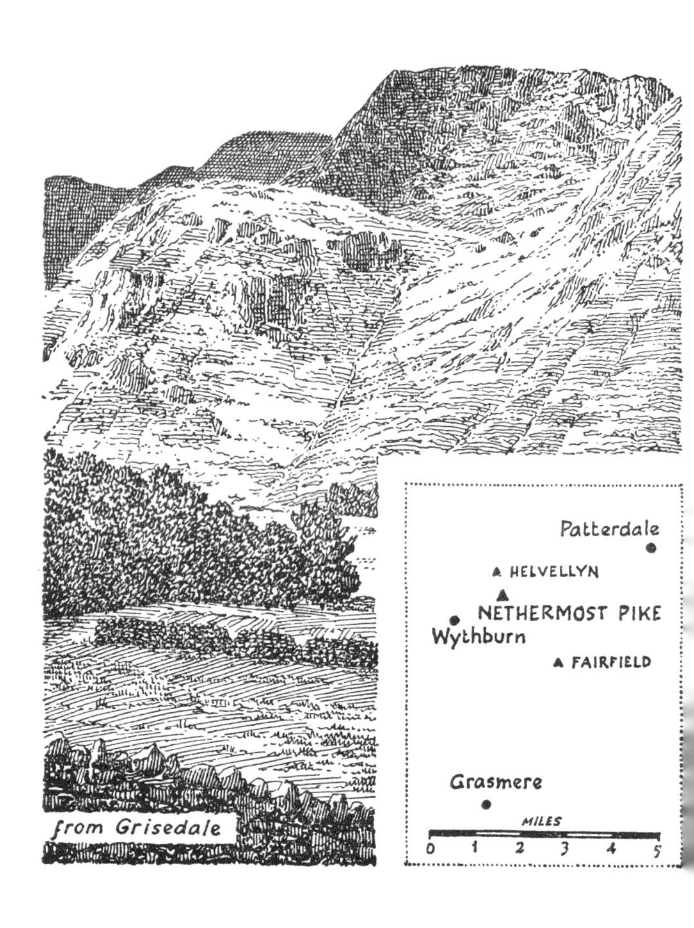

from Grisedale

From Book One

DATE/S WALKED

ASCENT/S USED

COMMENTS (walking companions, weather, etc.)

'Nethermost Pike is climbed incidentally, almost unknowingly, only because it is an obstacle in the route to Helvellyn. On the east side, however, is solitude, for here few men walk. Here, too, is a gem of a tarn.'

Pavey Ark

2288'

from the western slopes of Blea Rigg

From Book Three

DATE/S WALKED ....

....

....

ASCENT/S USED ....

....

....

COMMENTS (walking companions, weather, etc.) ....

....

....

....

....

....

....

....

....

....

....

....

....

....

'Seated comfortably with his back against the cairn, one leg pointing to Loughrigg Fell and the other to Lingmoor Fell, the walker finds reward for his toil, for between his feet is a gem of a view: that of Great Langdale's graceful curves and the long sylvan upper reach of Windermere.'

Pike o' Stickle

2323'

the second of the
Langdale Pikes

Pike OF Stickle,
to be correct

from Gimmer Crag

HIGH RAISE
PIKE O'
STICKLE
HARRISON
STICKLE
LOFT CRAG
New
Hotel
Old Hotel
Dungeon Ghyll
MILES
0 1 2 3

From Book Three

DATE/S WALKED ....

ASCENT/S USED ....

COMMENTS (walking companions, weather, etc.) ....

'Simple lines are often the most effective, and the smoothly-soaring pyramid of Pike o' Stickle, rising to a tapering thimble of rock without interruption or halt between valley or summit, is an imposing and impressive feature.'

Place Fell 2154'

Few fells are so well favoured as Place Fell for appraising neighbouring heights. It occupies an exceptionally good position in the curve of Ullswater, in the centre of a great bowl of hills; its summit commands a very beautiful and impressive panorama. On a first visit to Patterdale, Place Fell should be an early objective, for no other viewpoint gives such an appreciation of the design of this lovely corner of Lakeland.

From Book Two

DATE/S WALKED ....

....

....

ASCENT/S USED ....

....

....

COMMENTS (walking companions, weather, etc.) ....

....

....

....

....

....

....

....

....

....

....

....

....

....

'It is the author's opinion that the lakeside path from Scalehow Beck, near Sandwick, to Patterdale (in that direction) is the most beautiful and rewarding walk in Lakeland.'

Raise 2889'

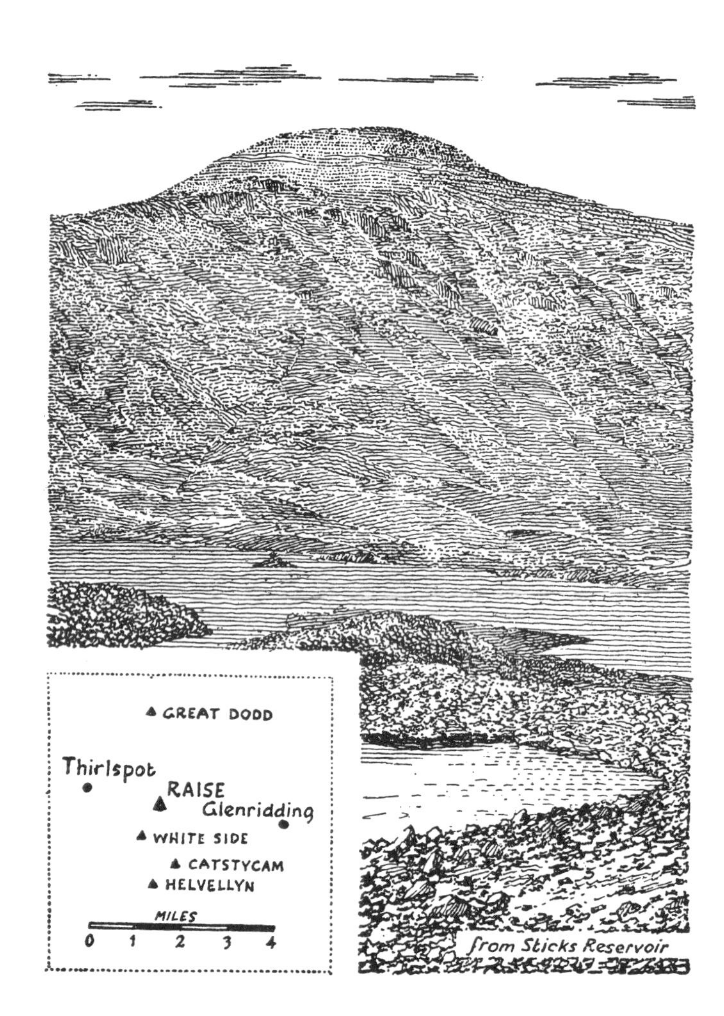

from Sticks Reservoir

From Book One

DATE/S WALKED

ASCENT/S USED

COMMENTS (walking companions, weather, etc.)

'Raise deserves a special cheer. It is the only summit in the Helvellyn range adorned with a crown of rough rocks – and they make a welcome change from the dull monotony of the green expanses around Sticks Pass.'

Rampsgill Head 2581'

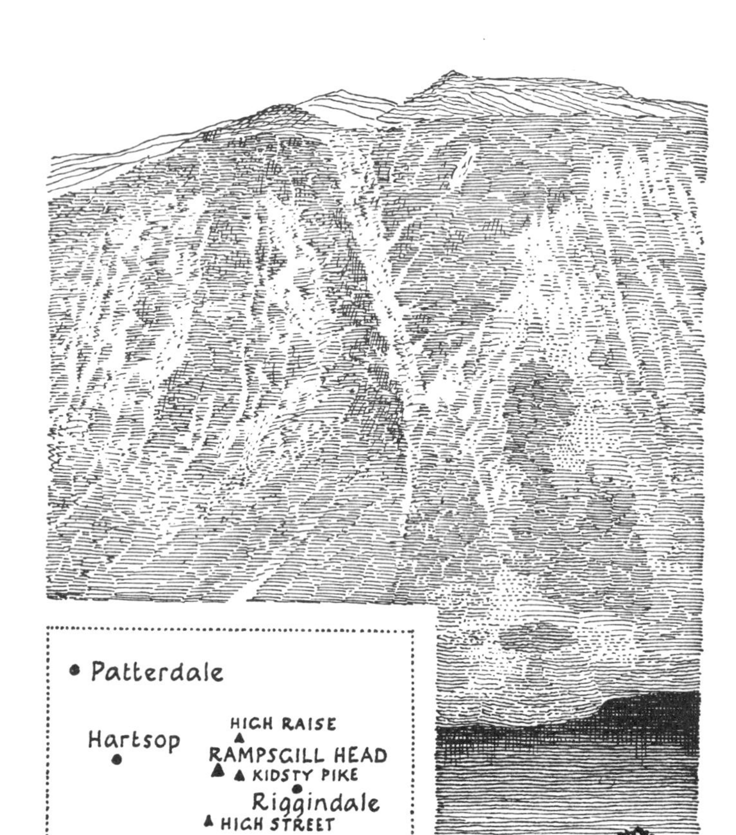

From Book Two

DATE/S WALKED ....

....

....

ASCENT/S USED ....

....

....

COMMENTS (walking companions, weather, etc.) ....

....

....

....

....

....

....

....

....

....

....

....

....

'On the right sort of day, the top is a pleasant place to linger awhile. The turf is delightful, there is some outcropping rock to add interest, the rim of crags is worthy of a leisurely and detailed exploration, the views are good in all directions.'

Raven Crag
1520' approx.
Dale Bottom
BLEABERRY FELL
Smeathwaite Bridge
RAVEN CRAG
HIGH SEAT
Armboth
MILES
0
1
2
3
4
from the Thirlmere dam

From Book Three

DATE/S WALKED

ASCENT/S USED

COMMENTS (walking companions, weather, etc.)

'Of the many dozens of Raven Crags in Lakeland, best known of all is this mighty buttress of grey rock towering above the Thirlmere dam. Its vertical face is a truly formidable object, standing out starkly from a dense surround of plantations.'

Red Screes 2541'

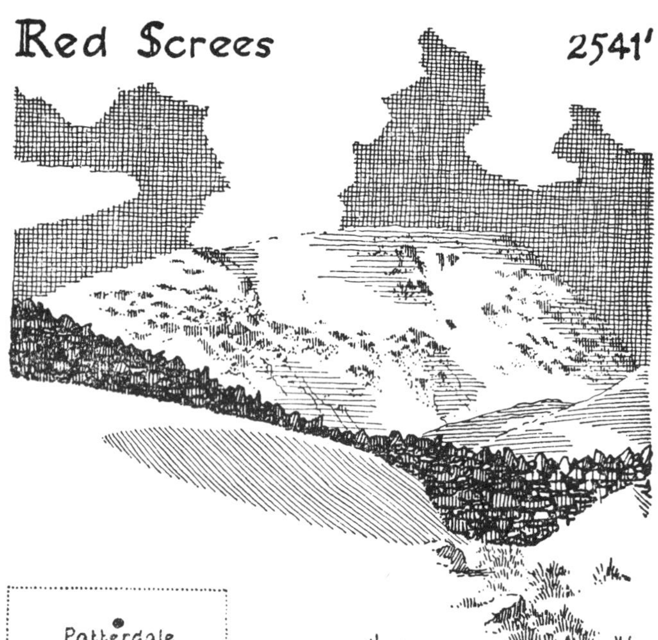

from Wansfell

Prominent in all views of the Lakeland fells from the lesser heights of South Westmorland is the high whale-backed mass of Red Screes, rising in a graceful curve from the head of Windermere and descending abruptly at its northern end. Some maps append the name 'Kilnshaw Chimney' to the summit, but Red Screes is its name by popular choice — and Red Screes it should be because of the colour and character of its eastern face. It is a friendly accommodating hill, holding no terrors for those who climb to its summit by the usual easy routes and being very conveniently situated for sojourners at Ambleside; moreover, it offers a reward of excellent views.

From Book One

DATE/S WALKED

ASCENT/S USED

COMMENTS (walking companions, weather, etc.)

'Below and east of the highest cairn on the summit is a prominent cluster of rocks worth visiting: it is a good vantage point, and a pleasant place to eat sandwiches if the top is crowded, but it is well to tread cautiously here: beware crag!'

Rest Dodd

2278'

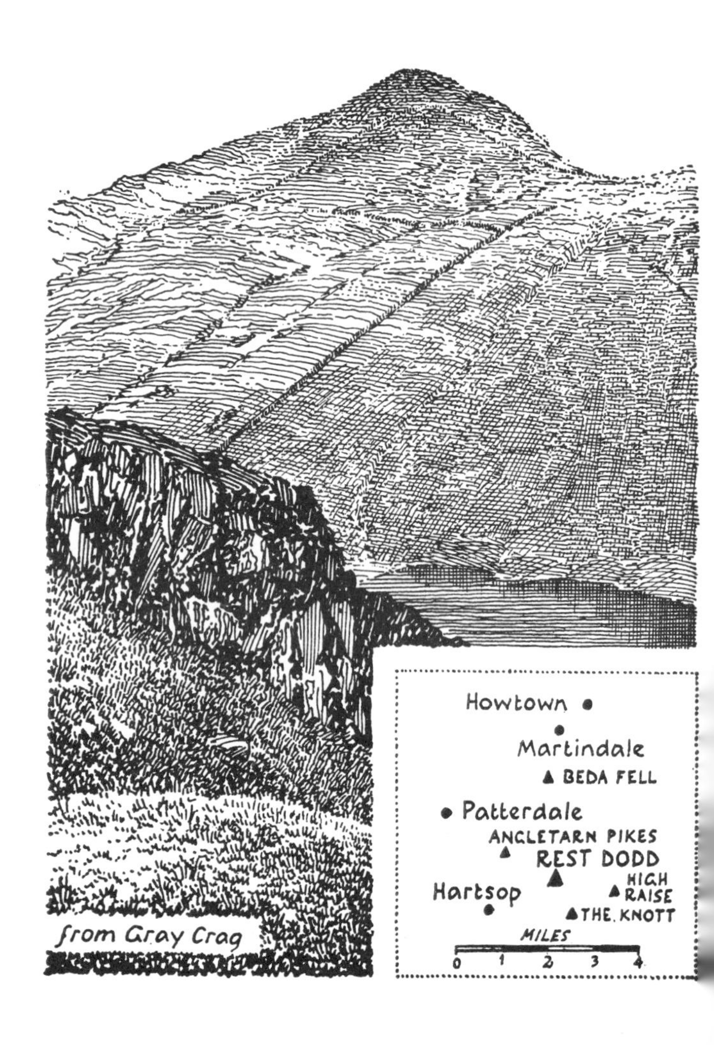

From Book Two

DATE/S WALKED ....

....

....

ASCENT/S USED ....

....

....

COMMENTS (walking companions, weather, etc.) ....

....

....

....

....

....

....

....

....

....

....

....

....

....

'Rest Dodd stands at an angle on the undulating grassy ridge coming down from the main watershed to the shores of Ullswater. Much of the fell is within the Martindale deer forest and out of bounds.'

Saint Sunday Crag   2756'

from Ullswater

From Book One

DATE/S WALKED

ASCENT/S USED

COMMENTS (walking companions, weather, etc.)

'Every walker who aspires to high places and looks up at the remote summit of St Sunday Crag will experience an urge to go forth and climb up to it, for its challenge is very strong. Saint Sunday must surely look down on his memorial with profound gratification.'

Sallows

1691'

better known locally
as Kentmere Park

from Badger Rock

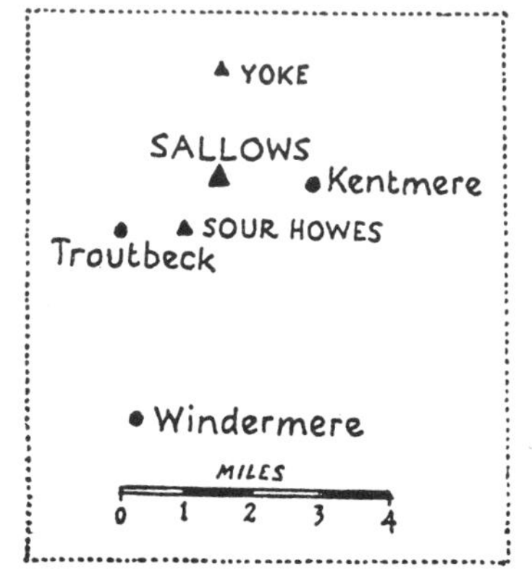

For most walkers, the fells proper in this region start at Garburn Pass and rise to the north, but there are two hills, twins almost, immediately to the south of the Pass, worth a mention although these are not strictly walkers' territory. The higher of the two is named Sallows (on all maps), bounding the Pass, and has much merit as a viewpoint and a scantier virtue as a grouse sanctuary. It is not worth the detour for anyone bound for Ill Bell and places north, and, in any case, there is not entirely free access to the fell and visitors may be requested to state their business

From Book Two

DATE/S WALKED ....

....

....

ASCENT/S USED ....

....

....

COMMENTS (walking companions, weather, etc.) ....

....

....

....

....

....

....

....

....

....

....

....

....

....

....

'The summit may be most easily and quickly visited from the top of Garburn Pass. Alternatively it can be gained by a mile-long ascent from the Ings–Kentmere Hall bridle-path.'

Seat Sandal 2415'

from Grasmere

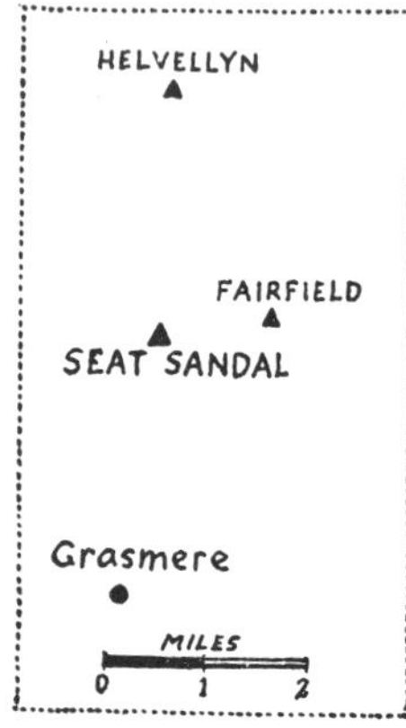

Cascade, Raise Beck

From Book One

DATE/S WALKED

ASCENT/S USED

COMMENTS (walking companions, weather, etc.)

'Prominent in the Grasmere landscape is the lofty outline of Seat Sandal, soaring gracefully from Dunmail Raise to the flat-topped summit and then suddenly falling away in a steep plunge eastwards.'

Selside Pike

2142'

from Mosedale Beck near the waterfalls

From Book Two

DATE/S WALKED

ASCENT/S USED

COMMENTS (walking companions, weather, etc.)

'One of the lesser-known fells is Selside Pike on the eastern fringe of the district, commanding the head of the shy and beautiful little valley of Swindale. For countless ages Selside Pike has looked down upon Swindale and seen there a picture of unspoiled charm.'

Sergeant Man 2414'

from Great Castle How

From Book Three

DATE/S WALKED ....

....

....

ASCENT/S USED ....

....

....

COMMENTS (walking companions, weather, etc.) ....

....

....

....

....

....

....

....

....

....

....

....

....

....

'The stones around the cairn have been scratched white by the nailed boots of visitors, testifying to the popularity of this summit. Sergeant Man is distinctive in having a stream within a furlong of the cairn, a point for specialists in mountain bivouacs to note.'

Sergeant's Crag 1873'

from Eagle Crag

From Book Three

DATE/S WALKED ....

....

....

ASCENT/S USED ....

....

....

COMMENTS (walking companions, weather, etc.) ....

....

....

....

....

....

....

....

....

....

....

....

....

....

'Sergeant's Crag is all rock and rough fell. The main crag, overlooking the valley, is a sheer wall of rock split by two gullies of which the more prominent was a favourite resort of climbers.'

Sheffield Pike 2232'

from Glenridding

From Book One

DATE/S WALKED

ASCENT/S USED

COMMENTS (walking companions, weather, etc.)

'Sheffield Pike soars abruptly between the valleys of Glenridding and Glencoyne and it presents to each a continuous fringe of steep crags. The eastern aspect is pleasing, with rock and heather and an occasional rowan mingling above well-wooded slopes.'

Shipman Knotts 1926'

from Stockdale

HARTER FELL
KENTMERE PIKE
TARN CRAG
ILL BELL
GREY CRAG
SHIPMAN KNOTTS
Kentmere
Longsleddale
0 1 2 3 4

Shipman Knotts is of moderate altitude and would have called for no more than the brief comment that it is a shoulder of Kentmere Pike had it not earned for itself a separate chapter by reason of the characteristic roughnesses of its surface. Rocky outcrops are everywhere on the steep slopes, persisting even in the woods of Sadgill, although these seldom attain the magnitude of crags. This fell is usually climbed on the way to Harter Fell from the south, and its rock should be welcomed for there is precious little beyond. The south slope carries the path from Kentmere to Longsleddale

From Book Two

DATE/S WALKED ....

....

....

ASCENT/S USED ....

....

....

COMMENTS (walking companions, weather, etc.) ....

....

....

....

....

....

....

....

....

....

....

....

....

....

'Shipman Knotts is usually climbed as a means of gaining access to the Harter Fell ridge, but is an interesting short expedition in itself. The cart-track linking Stile End and Sadgill is the regular highway between Kentmere and Longsleddale.'

Silver How 1292'

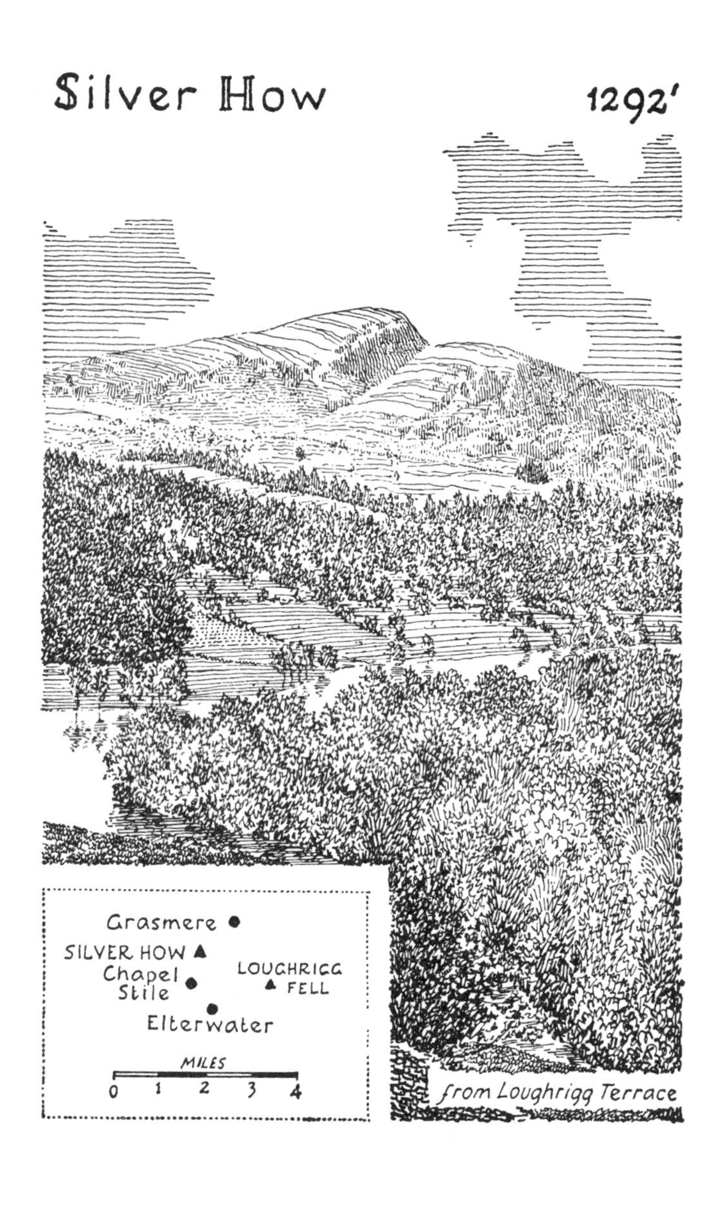

from Loughrigg Terrace

From Book Three

DATE/S WALKED

ASCENT/S USED

COMMENTS (walking companions, weather, etc.)

'A lovely name for a lovely fell: Silver How is delightful. It is the rough slopes that delight the eye, especially on the Grasmere side, for the intermingling of crag and conifer, juniper and bracken, is landscape artistry at its best.'

Sour Howes 1568'

better known locally as Applethwaite Common

from Troutbeck

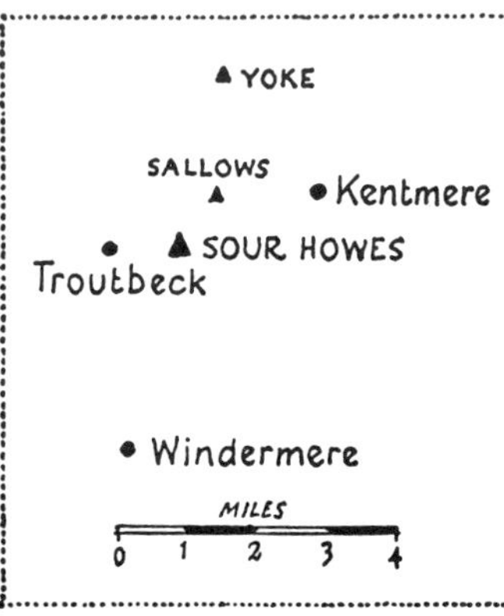

Although all maps agree that the summit of this fell is named Sour Howes, its broadest flank, carrying the Garburn Pass Road down to Troutbeck, is far better known as Applethwaite Common; this flank is traversed also by the pleasant Dubbs Road. There is little about the fell to attract walkers, and nothing to justify a detour from the main Ill Bell ridge to the north, for although the views are really good they are better from the main ridge. There is heather on the eastern slopes, and therefore, inevitably, grouse; and therefore, inevitably, shooting butts: one may admire the construction of these butts while deploring their purpose.

From Book Two

DATE/S WALKED ....

....

....

ASCENT/S USED ....

....

....

COMMENTS (walking companions, weather, etc.) ....

....

....

....

....

....

....

....

....

....

....

....

....

....

'The crowded skyline in the west arrests the attention, with the vertical profile of Scafell above Mickledore prominent in the scene. Langdale Pikes are well seen between and below Great End and Great Gable.'

Steel Fell 1811'

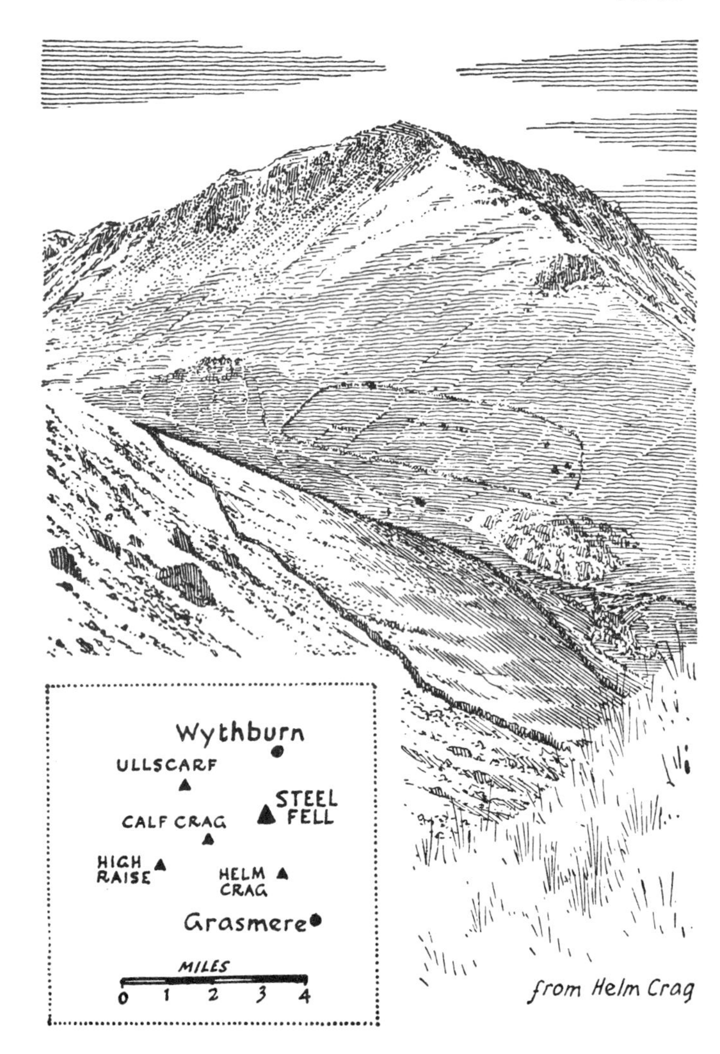

from Helm Crag

DATE/S WALKED

ASCENT/S USED

COMMENTS (walking companions, weather, etc.)

'The best scene unfolds to the north, where the noble Blencathra is a background to Thirlmere. To the southwest, lateral ridges rise to the skyline of the Coniston fells, all of them being of strikingly serrated appearance of Cuillin-like quality.'

Steel Knotts 1414'

summit named Pikeawassa

from Howe Grain Beck

Wether Hill's western flank swells into a bulge, Gowk Hill, which itself sends out a crooked bony arm northwards to form a lofty independent ridge running parallel to the main range and enclosing with it the short hidden valley of Fusedale. On the crest of this ridge, rock is never far from the surface and it breaks through in several places, notably at the highest point, which is a craggy tor that would worthily embellish the summit of many a higher fell. This freakish gnarled ridge is Steel Knotts; the summit-tor is named, on the best of authority, (but not by many, one imagines) Pikeawassa. *(O.S. 1" and 2½" maps)*

Howtown
STEEL KNOTTS
LOADPOT HILL
WETHER HILL
MILES
0 1 2 3

From Book Two

DATE/S WALKED ....

....

....

ASCENT/S USED ....

....

....

COMMENTS (walking companions, weather, etc.) ....

....

....

....

....

....

....

....

....

....

....

....

....

....

'Steel Knotts may well claim to have the sharpest summit in Lakeland, for the rock tor (Pikeawassa) that crowns the top is so acute that only very agile walkers will be able to stand upon it although, it will be noted, it is a popular perch for birds.'

Stone Arthur 1652'

sometimes referred to as Arthur's Chair

from Grasmere

▲ FAIRFIELD
▲ GREAT RIGG
▲ STONE ARTHUR
▲ HERON PIKE
Grasmere ▲ NAB SCAR
• Rydal
Ambleside
MILES
0 1 2 3 4

Without its prominent tor of steep rock, Stone Arthur would probably never have been given a name for it is merely the abrupt end of a spur of Great Rigg although it has the appearance of a separate fell when seen from Grasmere. The outcrop occurs where the gradual decline of the spur becomes pronounced and here are the short walls of rock, like a ruined castle, that give Stone Arthur its one touch of distinction.

From Book One

DATE/S WALKED ....

....

....

ASCENT/S USED ....

....

....

COMMENTS (walking companions, weather, etc.) ....

....

....

....

....

....

....

....

....

....

....

....

....

....

'The gem of the view is Easedale Tarn in its wild setting among colourful fells with a towering background culminating in Scafell Pike. The vale of Grasmere, below, is also attractive.'

Stybarrow Dodd

2770' approx.

from Brown Crag

Dockray
GREAT DODD
Stanah
STYBARROW DODD
Thirlspot
Glencoyne
RAISE
Glenridding
HELVELLYN
MILES
0 1 2 3 4

From Book One

DATE/S WALKED

ASCENT/S USED

COMMENTS (walking companions, weather, etc.)

'There is all the difference in the world between the two routes depicted. The direct way by Deep Dale is dreary and depressing; that by the Brown Hills is a splendid high-level route, excelling in its views of Ullswater below.'

Tarn Crag 2176'

from Sadgill Wood

From Book Two

DATE/S WALKED ....

....

....

ASCENT/S USED ....

....

....

COMMENTS (walking companions, weather, etc.) ....

....

....

....

....

....

....

....

....

....

....

....

....

....

'On a clear day there is an excellent panorama from the summit from east round to south – where, for a hundred miles, the noble skyline of the Pennines and the wide seascape of Morecambe Bay present themselves to view without obstruction.'

Tarn Crag 1801'

from Easedale Tarn

From Book Three

DATE/S WALKED

ASCENT/S USED

COMMENTS (walking companions, weather, etc.)

'The dominant feature in the rugged skyline around the head of Easedale Tarn is the arching curve of Tarn Crag, above a wild rocky slope that plunges very steeply to the dark waters at its base.'

Thornthwaite Crag 2569'

from Caudale Moor

From Book Two

DATE/S WALKED ....

....

....

ASCENT/S USED ....

....

....

COMMENTS (walking companions, weather, etc.) ....

....

....

....

....

....

....

....

....

....

....

....

....

....

'It is sometimes difficult to recall the details of familiar summits but surely all who have climbed Thornthwaite Crag will identify it in memory by its remarkable 14-feet column, one of the most distinctive cairns in Lakeland.'

Thunacar Knott 2351'

from Harrison Stickle

From north and south and east and west, Thunacar Knott is completely unphotogenic, and the best that any illustration can produce is a slight roughness of the slowly-swelling curve that forms its broad summit. This uninspiring characteristic extends to the whole fell, which is quite deficient in interest (if, as has already been decided for the purposes of this book, Pavey Ark is not regarded as a part of it, although it really is). Grey stones on the summit and spilling in patches down the easy slopes to Langstrath, do little to relieve the drab monotony of spacious sheep-walks. When fixing the county boundaries between Cumberland and Westmorland the surveyors decided that the demarcation should make a sharp angle on the top — which is probably the most exciting thing that ever happened to Thunacar Knott.

The upper valley of Stake Beck, draining the western slopes in a dreary landscape of moraines, may yet bring a belated fame to the fell, for preliminary searches here suggest it as a likely area of activity by neolithic man.

From Book Three

DATE/S WALKED

ASCENT/S USED

COMMENTS (walking companions, weather, etc.)

'The fell has two tops, with a tarn occupying the slight depression between. The recognised summit, surmounted by a well-made cairn, is a mound north of the tarn (which has interesting amphibious plant growth).'

Troutbeck Tongue 1191'

properly named
The Tongue, Troutbeck Park

from the Kirkstone-Windermere road

CAUDALE MOOR
ILL BELL
TROUTBECK TONGUE
Troutbeck
MILES
0 1 2 3

There are many Tongues in Lakeland, all of them wedges of high or rising ground between enclosing becks that join below at the tip, but none is more distinctive or aptly named than that in the middle of the Troutbeck Valley. Other Tongues usually have their roots high on a mountainside, but this one thrusts forward from the floor of the dalehead. Although of very modest altitude, it has an attraction for the gentler pedestrian as a viewpoint for the valley, and makes an admirable short excursion in pleasant scenery from Windermere or Troutbeck or, by Skelghyll Woods, from Ambleside.

From Book Two

DATE/S WALKED

ASCENT/S USED

COMMENTS (walking companions, weather, etc.)

'Troutbeck Tongue is set deep in the bottom of a great bowl of hills, all of which overtop it and limit the scene. Only to the south is there an open view – of Windermere – but there is also a peep of distant fells to the west.'

Ullscarf 2370'

from Great Crag
Watendlath Fell

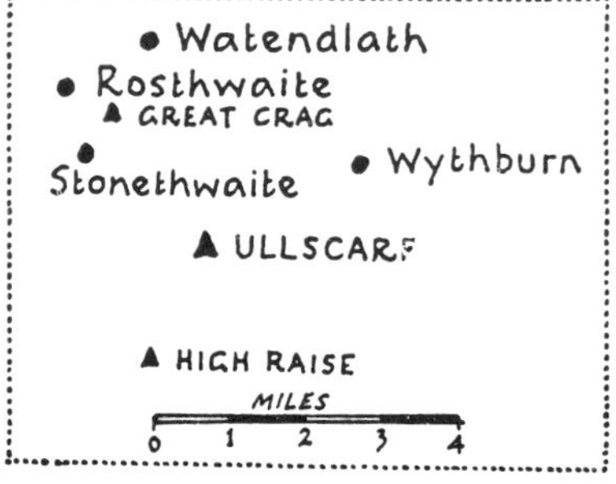

Binka Stone
near Dobgill Bridge

From Book Three

DATE/S WALKED

ASCENT/S USED

COMMENTS (walking companions, weather, etc.)

'Of the Lakeland fells over 2000 feet, Ullscarf will generally be adjudged the most central, and it is a pity that Nature has not endowed it with a distinctive superstructure worthy of the honour. The most central, perhaps, but not, alas, a very distinguished pivot!'

Walla Crag

1234'

'Wallow Crag' on old editions of Ordnance Survey maps

Some walkers have difficulty in remembering the altitudes of the fells. There is no excuse here for anybody who can count up to four.

from Falcon Crag

from near Rakefoot

From Book Three

DATE/S WALKED ....

....

....

ASCENT/S USED ....

....

....

COMMENTS (walking companions, weather, etc.) ....

....

....

....

....

....

....

....

....

....

....

....

....

....

'A delectable place for a picnic, the heathery top of Walla Crag is also a favourite viewpoint for Derwentwater, seen directly below the long steep escarpment. Borrowdale is an outstanding study of mountain grouping.'

Wansfell 1597'

From Book Two

DATE/S WALKED

ASCENT/S USED

COMMENTS (walking companions, weather, etc.)

'Although the summit ridge of Wansfell is fairly narrow and well-defined, the slopes on most sides are extensive, the fell as a whole occupying a broad tract of territory between Ambleside and the Troutbeck valley.'

Watson's Dodd 2584'

From Book One

DATE/S WALKED

ASCENT/S USED

COMMENTS (walking companions, weather, etc.)

'A few big stones adorn the highest point, and they look strangely alien just there, as though they had been carried there. (Maybe Mr Watson undertook this task: if so, it is fitting that the fell should bear his name.)'

Wether Hill

2210'
approx

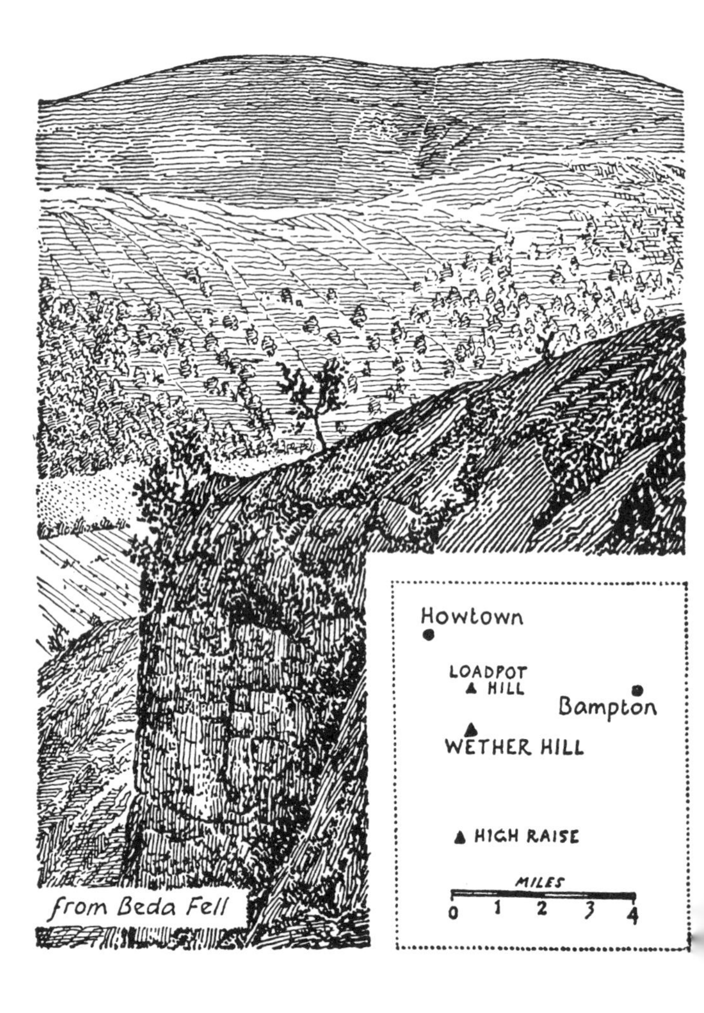

From Book Two

DATE/S WALKED ....

....

....

ASCENT/S USED ....

....

....

COMMENTS (walking companions, weather, etc.) ....

....

....

....

....

....

....

....

....

....

....

....

....

....

'The best features of Wether Hill are found in its valleys: eastwards, Cawdale Beck and Measand Beck have attractions rarely visited except by the lone shepherd; westwards, Fusedale Beck is fed from two wooded ravines, and here too is lovely Martindale.'

White Side 2832'

— a name of convenience.
The summit is strictly nameless, White Side being the west slope below the top (probably so-called from splashes of quartz on many of the stones).

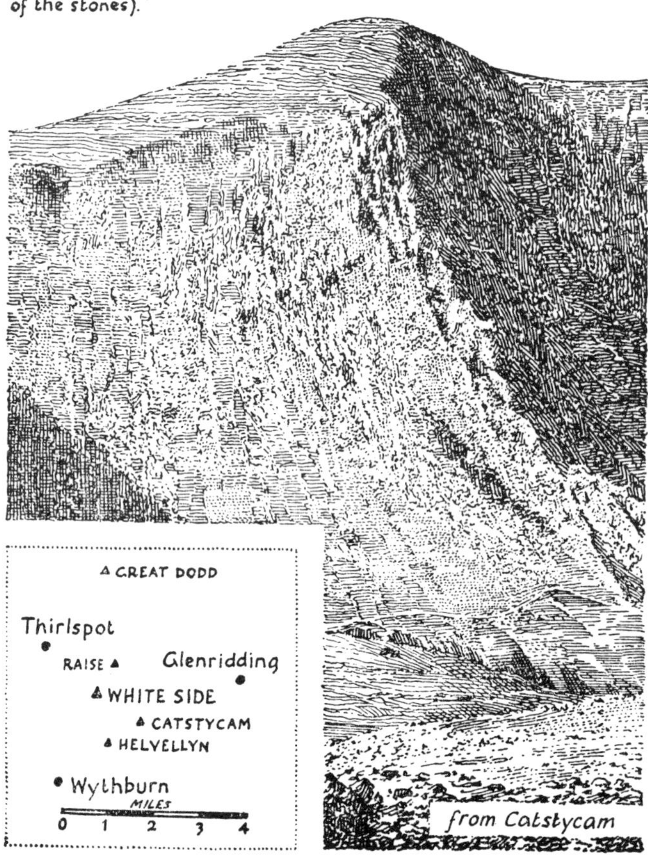

from Catstycam

From Book One

DATE/S WALKED

ASCENT/S USED

COMMENTS (walking companions, weather, etc.)

'Although White Side presents an intimidating wall of low crags to travellers on the road at Thirlspot, its upper slopes on this western side are docile enough, being wholly of grass at easy gradients. Skiers and sheep share a high regard for White Side.'

Yoke

2309'

spelt 'Yolk' on some Ordnance Survey maps

from the Kirkstone-Windermere road

From Book Two

DATE/S WALKED

ASCENT/S USED

COMMENTS (walking companions, weather, etc.)

'The Kentmere flank of Yoke abounds in interest. Below the summit is the formidable thousand-foot precipice of Rainsborrow Crag (the safety of which is a subject of disagreement between rock-climbers and foxes).'

ADDITIONAL NOTES (1)

ADDITIONAL NOTES (2)

ADDITIONAL NOTES (3)

ADDITIONAL NOTES (4)

ADDITIONAL NOTES (5)

ADDITIONAL NOTES (6)

ADDITIONAL NOTES (7)

ADDITIONAL NOTES (8)

ADDITIONAL NOTES (9)

ADDITIONAL NOTES (10)

ADDITIONAL NOTES (11)

ADDITIONAL NOTES (12)

ADDITIONAL NOTES (13)

ADDITIONAL NOTES (14)

ADDITIONAL NOTES (15)

ADDITIONAL NOTES (16)

ADDITIONAL NOTES (17)

ADDITIONAL NOTES (18)

ADDITIONAL NOTES (19)

ADDITIONAL NOTES (20)

ADDITIONAL NOTES (21)